W9-ABN-787

LIVES OF GREAT RELIGIOUS BOOKS

The Jefferson Bible

LIVES OF GREAT RELIGIOUS BOOKS

The Jefferson Bible, Peter Manseau
The Passover Haggadah, Vanessa Ochs
Josephus's *The Jewish War*, Martin Goodman
The *Song of Songs*, Ilana Pardes
The Life of Saint Teresa of Avila, Carlos Eire
The Book of *Exodus*, Joel S. Baden
The Book of *Revelation*, Timothy Beal
The *Talmud*, Barry Scott Wimpfheimer
The *Koran* in English, Bruce B. Lawrence
The *Lotus Sūtra*, Donald S. Lopez, Jr.
John Calvin's *Institutes of the Christian Religion*, Bruce Gordon
C. S. Lewis's *Mere Christianity*, George M. Marsden
The *Bhagavad Gita*, Richard H. Davis
The *Yoga Sutra of Patanjali*, David Gordon White
Thomas Aquinas's *Summa theologiae*, Bernard McGinn
The *Book of Common Prayer*, Alan Jacobs
The Book of *Job*, Mark Larrimore
The *Dead Sea Scrolls*, John J. Collins
The Book of *Genesis*, Ronald Hendel
The *Book of Mormon*, Paul C. Gutjahr
The *I Ching*, Richard J. Smith
The Tibetan Book of the Dead, Donald S. Lopez, Jr.
Augustine's *Confessions*, Garry Wills
Dietrich Bonhoeffer's *Letters and Papers from Prison*, Martin E. Marty

The Jefferson Bible

A BIOGRAPHY

Peter Manseau

PRINCETON UNIVERSITY PRESS

Princeton and Oxford

Requests for permission to reproduce material from this work
should be sent to permissions@press.princeton.edu

Published by Princeton University Press
41 William Street, Princeton, New Jersey 08540
6 Oxford Street, Woodstock, Oxfordshire OX20 1TR

press.princeton.edu

Library of Congress Control Number: 2020939834

All Rights Reserved
ISBN 9780691205694
ISBN (e-book) 9780691209685

British Library Cataloging-in-Publication Data is available

Editorial: Fred Appel and Jenny Tan
Production Editorial: Debbie Tegarden
Jacket/Cover Design: Lorraine Doneker
Production: Erin Suydam
Publicity: James Schneider and Kathryn Stevens
Copyeditor: Michelle Garceau

Jacket/Cover Credit: *The Life and Morals of Jesus of Nazareth*, sample
page of four text columns. Courtesy of the Smithsonian Institution

This book has been composed in Garamond Premier Pro

Printed on acid-free paper. ∞

Printed in the United States of America

10 9 8 7 6 5 4 3 2 1

CONTENTS

LIST OF ILLUSTRATIONS   vii

AUTHOR'S NOTE AND
    ACKNOWLEDGMENTS   ix

INTRODUCTION   Excavating the Sacred   1

CHAPTER 1   Sharpening the Blade   15

CHAPTER 2   Making the Cut   31

CHAPTER 3   The Quest for the Jeffersonian Jesus   55

CHAPTER 4   Lost and Found   74

CHAPTER 5   Born Again   95

CHAPTER 6   Social Engineering   118

CHAPTER 7   Congressional Inheritances   134

CHAPTER 8   Jefferson, Jesus, and the Sixties   147

CHAPTER 9   Choose Your Own Adventure   165

EPILOGUE   Bible as Barrow   179

ILLUSTRATIONS   185

NOTES   193

INDEX   211

LIST OF ILLUSTRATIONS

FIGURE 1 The Life and Morals of Jesus of Nazareth,
title page   187

FIGURE 2 The Life and Morals of Jesus of Nazareth,
index   188

FIGURE 3 The Life and Morals of Jesus of Nazareth,
four text columns   189

FIGURE 4 New Testament source book   190

FIGURE 5 Cyrus Adler   191

FIGURE 6 John Fletcher Lacey   192

Entwined with legend, lore, and guesswork, theories concerning the purpose of the barrows proliferated throughout the middle of the eighteenth century. Accounts of battles fought in their vicinity inspired the belief among some that these mounds were accidental monuments to the war dead, covered over with soil on the spots where they fell. Others maintained that the custom of the local Monacan people called for periodically disinterring corpses from far-flung graves to be gathered and reburied ritually in a single location which had been sanctified for that purpose. Perhaps the most haunting explanation of the barrows was that they were "general sepulchres" for entire villages that no longer existed. According to a tradition "said to be handed down from the aboriginal Indians," Jefferson wrote:

> when they settled in a town, the first person who died was placed erect, and earth put about him, so as to cover and support him. . . . When another died, a narrow passage was dug to the first, the second reclined against him, and the cover of earth replaced, and so on.

Each mound was thus a reminder that all that remained of once thriving communities were their mortal remains, standing together as if in conversation just beneath the surface of a vibrant green hill.

"I wished to satisfy myself whether any, and which of these opinions were just," Jefferson explained. And so he set off to the low grounds of the Rivana River, "opposite some hills, on which had been an Indian town." There he encountered "a spheroidical form," which he estimated had once been forty feet wide and twelve feet high. By the time Jefferson got to it, much of the mound had long been under

Excavating the Sacred

Before he had been gripped by a desire to remake his country, young Thomas Jefferson was moved by a different kind of interest in the land of his birth: a hunger to uncover all that might be learned from the American earth. From an early age, he rarely minded getting his hands dirty. In addition to his brief stint as an official surveyor for Albemarle County, Virginia, and the many agricultural experiments performed with the help of enslaved labor at Monticello, Jefferson was known to undertake works of archaeological excavation, putting shovels and pickaxes to the service of science.

As he wrote in the one book he published during his lifetime, 1785's *Notes on the State of Virginia*, Jefferson was fascinated by grass-covered mounds called barrows which, he noted, could be "found all over this country," including in the rolling Piedmont landscape he had explored since childhood.[1]

> These are of different sizes, some of them constructed of earth, and some of loose stones. That they were repositories of the dead has been obvious to all; but on what particular occasion constructed was matter of doubt.

cultivation, and so had been reduced by the plough to around seven feet, just over the height of a tall man like Jefferson himself.

Eager to see what was inside this barrow, the young excavator went to work. His findings were as immediate as they were macabre.

> I first dug superficially in several parts of it, and came to collections of human bones, at different depths, from six inches to three feet below the surface. These were lying in the utmost confusion, some vertical, some oblique, some horizontal, and directed to every point of the compass, entangled, and held together in clusters by the earth.

Jefferson's orderly mind was apparently offended by the jumble he had discovered, which could not have been further from the image of a carefully arranged convening of the dead.

> Bones of the most distant parts were found together, as, for instance, the small bones of the foot in the hollow of a scull, many sculls would sometimes be in contact, lying on the face, on the side, on the back, top or bottom, so as on the whole to give the idea of bones emptied promiscuously from a bag or basket, and covered over with earth, without any attention to their order.

Along with "sculls," he catalogued "the bones of the arms, thighs, legs, feet, and hands." There were also jawbones, teeth, ribs, and vertebrae from the neck and the spine.

It was the skulls that most drew Jefferson's interest. Some were "so tender," he noted, that they fell apart at the touch, leaving him with a handful of teeth that were considerably smaller than others. At least one section of the mound seemed to include children—a suspicion reinforced by the discoveries that followed: "a rib and a fragment of the under jaw of a person about half grown; another rib of an infant, and part of the jaw of a child, which had not yet cut its teeth." These bones were white; all the others more the color of sand.

"The bones of infants being soft, they probably decay sooner," Jefferson surmised, "which might be the cause so few were found here." Though he had apparently gathered such bones in sufficient quantity that he remarked he was "particular in my attention" to them, as his work continued, the remains of children accounted for only a small fraction of the total number of skeletons in the barrow, which he supposed "might have been a thousand."

When Jefferson's work was done, the man occasionally called "the Father of American Archaeology" for this excavation announced his opinion that the mound was not the buried site of a battle, or a meticulously arranged sepulcher, but rather a cemetery formed across time and generations, with strata of remains that appeared more recent the closer to the surface they were found. He also knew that this formation was not a matter of ancient history, but of ongoing interest to those for whom the bones within were something more than specimens to be recorded in a naturalist's notebook.[2]

"On whatever occasion they may have been made," Jefferson wrote of the barrows, "they are of considerable notoriety among the Indians." He had once seen a group of Monacans leave a high road and descend six miles into the forest to visit a mound, "without any instructions or enquiry," most likely in remembrance of those buried there.

While he had cut into the mound with the same joyful spirit of inquiry he later applied to so many of his pursuits, the Monacans "staid about it some time, with expressions which were construed to be those of sorrow."

* * *

It is an object lesson in changing attitudes concerning what makes something sacred that today the image of Jefferson rummaging through the bones of Native Americans would likely be regarded by many as an obvious desecration, while in his own day it would have been praised as a purely scientific endeavour. This should come as little surprise. Notions of what constitutes that which ought to be inviolable may alter significantly from one generation to the next, to say nothing of the changes that occur across centuries. Taking stock of how this is so can be a useful measure of a society's transforming concerns. Traffic between the controversial and the commonplace runs in both directions, and the transit of each within the American context offers insight into who Americans were at the time of the nation's founding, who they have been throughout its history, and who they are now.

Opinions have similarly changed concerning another dramatic act of excavation undertaken by Jefferson in Virginia, which likewise has struck some as a defilement and others merely as the work of a mind moved by reason alone. That would be, of course, the subject of this book: the hand-crafted, cut-and-paste, compressed version of the Gospels edited by Jefferson with a sharp blade and glue; a book he called *The Life and Morals of Jesus of Nazareth* but is more commonly known as the Jefferson Bible.

Extricating biblical passages he found instructive and useful from those he did not, Jefferson dug into the scripture most of his countrymen took for granted as the word of God no less zealously than he had into the burial barrows near his home. Doing so was the enactment of his long planned intention to extract the teachings of Jesus of Nazareth—"a system of the most sublime morality which has ever fallen from the lips of man"—from the "dross of his biographers," which to Jefferson accounted for the majority of the New Testament's text.[3] On more than one occasion, Jefferson referred to his desire to differentiate the words of Jesus from those of others claiming to speak for him in colorful language evoking both discovery and disdain.

"It is as easy to separate those parts," Jefferson wrote to John Adams in 1814, "as to pick out diamonds from dunghills."[4]

As bookends of his adulthood—the barrow digging occurring as a young man, and the Bible cutting in his dotage—these two acts of excavation have a surprising amount in common, and together say much about the third president and his times.

Each effort was methodical, meticulous, and seemingly unconcerned with conventional squeamishness, superstition, or notions of propriety. Each, in other words, might be seen as a practical application of the ideals of the Enlightenment. Each also was undertaken to correct misapprehensions of history. In the case of the barrows, Jefferson hoped to consider and discount local legends that obscured rather than revealed the American past. In the case of the Gospels, he hoped to show how true Christianity, too, had been hidden over time by misinformation. To Jefferson, the Jesus of history was buried as surely as bones of the Monacan dead, not by Virginia dirt and stone but by the sedimentary layers of centuries-old religious tradition, which the founding iconoclast elsewhere dismissed summarily as the "abracadabra of the mountebanks calling themselves the priests of Jesus."[5]

And yet, for Jefferson, only one of these excavations was an act suitable for putting before the public, and remarkably it was the one which found him poking at the skulls of children until they crumbled in his hands. News that he had devoted more than a decade of his life to plotting how he might dismantle the Bible, he suspected, would be a bridge too far—or, to use a more apt cliché, digging his own grave.

Though he was a man who took up his pen against empire and crown, Jefferson knew that taking a blade to the New Testament's pages would lend credence to suspicions that he was an infidel, a heretic, or worse. His Bible redaction was a project which he had long considered, but had discussed with only a few trusted correspondents. Jefferson made no plans to publish it and consented to have an early outline printed only when given assurance that his name would be in no way associated with its publication. By some accounts he read from *The Life and Morals of Jesus of Nazareth* nightly, and yet it seems he hoped virtually no one would know it existed. Perhaps the last monumental work of a monumental life, the Jefferson Bible is an ambivalent scripture that has taken on an outsized significance in a nation for which religious ambivalence is the one enduring creed.

* * *

But is it a great religious book?

Some might say it is hardly a book at all. Though the original is bound in fine red leather, and its published print and electronic editions now number in the dozens, it is ultimately a collage. Jefferson wrote barely a word of its content, but rather gathered passages written by many others in four languages across two millennia. He reordered the passages with little regard for the intention with which they were first composed, repurposing them rather according to his own intuition and sensibilities. The Dadaists might have recognized it as a *découpé*. Had it come from the desk of William Burroughs a generation later, it would have been called a cut-up. Today, the most appropriate analogue for what Jefferson accomplished might be music sampling. Made up of sound-bites of scripture separated, shuffled, and stitched back together in a way that seeks to supplant rather than serve their original meaning, the Jefferson Bible is less a book than a remix.

And yet, simultaneously, it is many books. It is at once the single physical volume that Jefferson created, and which now resides in the collections of the Smithsonian Institution's National Museum of American History, and it is the multiple volumes he used as raw material, most lost to history, two of which are similarly found in the museum, preserving perfectly the words he left behind. So, too, it is the many different editions of Jefferson's redaction, which cumulatively have sold hundreds of thousands of copies since its first publication more than a century ago. Each later edition might be seen as a book distinct from the others, and each draws selectively upon the larger corpus of Jeffersonian thought, quoting his piquant correspondence related to the project in order to frame Jefferson's gospel with epistles and apocrypha supportive of dramatically different interpretations of the primary text.

A critique one often hears regarding the common practice of referring to this work as "The Jefferson Bible" is that Jefferson had no intention of crafting a Bible of his own and would have objected to his redaction project being so named. Yet we can see here a distinction that must be made. Indeed, it is true that although Jefferson sought only to create a work he entitled *The Life and Morals of Jesus of Nazareth*, a work appropriately called the Jefferson Bible no less certainly has been formed. Just as the Bible itself was not composed so much as collected, edited, and remade over time, so too the Jefferson Bible is not limited to the original text, but also includes what has become of it.

While the singular, cut-and-paste *The Life and Morals of Jesus of Nazareth* remains static, the Jefferson Bible has been given new meanings with each generation, new arguments and understandings of what Jefferson did and why. If it is true that, as Jefferson said, "the tree of liberty must be refreshed from time to time with the blood of patriots and tyrants," it seems that the same might be said of the Jefferson Bible and ink.[6] The words of course remain the same (for the most part, as we shall see), but then one marker of religious books, great and otherwise, is that the words they contain are not always the point. As with other culturally important sacred tomes, the greatness of the Jefferson Bible can perhaps be found less in the text itself than in what it signifies. It is less a book to be read than to be talked about. In fact, as much of the published commentary about the Jefferson Bible suggests, some have talked at great length about it without apparently having read much of it at all.

As *The Life and Morals of Jesus of Nazareth* marks the 200th anniversary of its completion in 2020, the Jefferson

Bible begins its third century as an unlikely spiritual and historical Rorschach test. Illuminating both the third president's religious views and changing public opinion on the place of religion in American life, it is a text that inspires more questions than it answers. Is the homespun 84-page volume evidence that the Founding Fathers actively engaged with scripture, using its lessons to help birth a Christian nation? Or does it prove, on the contrary, that the Framers of the Republic sought to root out the stubborn influence of faith, the better to foster a new secular order? Was it merely the strange retirement project of an idiosyncratic statesman, or did it represent a broader cultural shift in the young United States away from ecclesial authority and toward the ideals of the Enlightenment?

The Jefferson Bible has done all this and more. Completed six years before his death, it is a slim assemblage of roughly one thousand New Testament verses, in English, French, Greek, and Latin, each cut carefully by Jefferson's own hand and then pasted meticulously on blank paper to craft a condensed version of the Gospels. It is a uniquely American testament shorn, for the most part, of its miraculous and supernatural elements; a Bible in which the sage of Monticello could believe without qualifications.

With the ideas behind its composition first quickening in Jefferson during the early years of Independence, the book has a history parallel to that of the nation. Some seven decades after its composition, its rediscovery and popularization late in the nineteenth century by the U.S. National Museum made the Jefferson Bible part of American self-understanding in a way that can be claimed for few other books. The stories of its creation, publication, and the uses to which it has been put—its birth, life, and afterlife—each occur within the context of a country and its people engaged in moments of transformation, as they were attempting to carve new identities from established traditions, much as Jefferson wielded his blade.

This biography of *The Life and Morals of Jesus of Nazareth* will explore not just how and why the text was edited and arranged by Jefferson, but also the many ways in which it has been presented, discussed, and reframed over time. The aim here is to reconsider the text within the various contexts that have contributed to its enduring allure while also providing a close reading of the Jefferson Bible itself.

Since it became widely known to the public in the 1890s, there have been more than two dozen printed editions of *The Life and Morals of Jesus of Nazareth*. The first official publication, the 1904 production of the US Government Printing Office, is a photographic facsimile of the original, with a brief introduction by Cyrus Adler, Librarian of the Smithsonian, Director of the U.S. National Museum's Division of Religion, and the man most responsible for bringing the book to light.[7] While its publication was first planned for distribution only to members of Congress, variant editions for other interested readers appeared almost immediately—indeed, even before the official publication.[8] It was, after all, exceedingly easy to follow Jefferson's edits to create new renditions of the same redacted texts. By the 1920s there were five editions in circulation, both as cheap pocket-sized books and as collectors' items, in formats ranging from photo-plates, to typeset text, to an entirely new translation. Two decades later, a popular commercial edition edited and introduced by the New York publishing executive and self-help writer Douglas Lurton (author of *The Power of Positive Living: Everyday Psychology for Getting What You Want Out of Life*) packaged the book as a simplified telling of "the most exquisite story ever written."[9] A generation after that, several editions viewed the text through the lens of the political turmoil of the 1960s and 70s, before it received its first and still unsurpassed scholarly treatment when it was prepared for inclusion in Princeton University Press's *Papers of Thomas Jefferson* series. After the death of two editors, Dickinson Adams in 1977 and Julian Boyd in 1980, *Jefferson's Extracts from the Gospels* finally saw publication in 1983.[10] Throughout this same period, a number of Unitarian Universalist ministers (and the American Unitarian Association-founded Beacon Press) claimed the book as their own with introductions connecting Jefferson's work with U.U. doctrine and history; this marked the most persuasive of efforts by religious and non-religious groups to conscript the Jefferson Bible into a cause.[11] Most recently, in furtherance of the Smithsonian Institution's mission of the "increase and diffusion of knowledge," in 2011 my colleagues at the National Museum of American History produced a full-color facsimile edition to commemorate the book's newly completed conservation and exhibition at the museum. It is this edition to which I will refer when quoting directly from *The Life and Morals of Jesus of Nazareth*.[12]

There has been a new Jefferson Bible for every generation since its discovery. The shared assumption of each of these editions has been that the significance of the book is found mainly in the text itself and the man who created it.

But, in fact, the Jefferson Bible is not one text but many; it has no single author but a cast of editors, publishers, champions, and critics who together made a twentieth-century publishing phenomenon out of a nineteenth-century assemblage of materials that trace their origin to the first century. It is a book whose relevance has been continually questioned, refashioned, and renewed, much like the man who first made it.

From the point of view of American religious history, the story of the Jefferson Bible's reception may be more important than its inception. It continues to speak about religion's role in our national mythology, and it always finds something new to say.

As with Jefferson's barrows, the meaning of the Jefferson Bible—as a cut-up text, as a cultural artifact, as a relic of the founding fathers, as a publishing mainstay—requires some excavation. It is often covered over with, as Jefferson said of Jesus's words in the New Testament, the "dross of his biographers," which now measure centuries deep. The goal of this biography of the book is to dig into its history in a way that has not been attempted before, with the aims both of taking a close look at what lies beneath while also examining the layers of meaning that have created the current impression of Jefferson and his Bible.

The chapters that follow are for the most part chronological, tracing the conception, birth, life, and afterlife of *The Life and Morals of Jesus of Nazareth*. Yet adherence to chronology will not be strict. Jefferson's blade was a time machine of sorts, a tool for revisiting the ancient past for the purpose of providing a corrective to centuries of tradition.

The scrapbook he made is, among all its other meanings, a record of that journey. Though this book is not nearly so ambitious, it too hopes to point toward multiple historical moments simultaneously, all pivoting around the instant when the knife first met the page.

Sharpening the Blade

During much of Thomas Jefferson's lifetime, heresy was a crime with potentially dire consequences. Echoes of English laws that had first called for the burning of "divers false and perverse people" sharing "wicked doctrine and heretical and erroneous opinions" under the writ of *De heretico combu-rendo* in 1401, remained on the books in Virginia until 1776, when the commonwealth's General Assembly "repealed all Acts of Parliament which had rendered criminal the maintaining [of] any opinions in matters of religion."[1]

No one was ever executed in Virginia for "wicked doctrine," but that did not mean religious behavior was not scrupulously policed. The Anglican establishment into which Jefferson was born, and in which he readily played his part in adulthood as a vestryman, maintained its authority by creating obstacles to dissent. Along with laws such as those threatening death for bringing a single Quaker into the colony, Virginians faced scrutiny not just for their actions but also their motivations and beliefs. As Jefferson lamented:

> By our own act of assembly of 1705, if a person brought up in the Christian religion denies the being of a God, or

the Trinity, or asserts there are more Gods than one, or denies the Christian religion to be true, or the scriptures to be of divine authority, he is punishable on the first offence by incapacity to hold any office or employment ecclesiastical, civil, or military; on the second by disability to sue, to take any gift or legacy, to be guardian, executor, or administrator, and by three years imprisonment, without bail.[2]

To deny the divine authority of scripture—to suggest that the Bible was crafted by human hands, that it was shaped by history, circumstance, and perhaps even by ignorance and error—was to court the scorn of one's neighbors and the punishment of the state. What sort of man born in such an environment would dare put a knife edge to a single page of sacred text?

Remarkably, it was one with the least controversial religious upbringing imaginable. As is frequently said to explain this champion of freedom's ownership of enslaved people, Jefferson was a man of his times. Those times included a widespread reevaluation of religious authority which allowed a boy born in the Virginia woods access to the Enlightenment thinking that was then remaking the world's churches and nations. The leaders and exemplars of these movements would prove to be the spiritual whetstones against which Jefferson sharpened the blade of his intellect.

As the late dean of American historians of religion Edwin Gaustad put it, Jefferson not only was raised in an "Anglican ambience," he "began life as an Anglican and ended it the same way." Most likely baptized at home, as other Virginian gentry like George Washington and George

Mason were, Jefferson was from infancy a conventional Christian of the established church, who likely would have been scandalized by the suggestion that one day he would presume to make a Bible of his own.[3]

Yet even in his youth Jefferson seems also to have had a sense that religious texts have a practical dimension and might be put to novel ends. His nineteenth-century biographer Harry Randall mentions that Jefferson's second earliest memory was of being a toddler upset when dinner was delayed one night. Though no plate was set before him, he recited the Lord's Prayer as a grace before the meal. In this act Jefferson hoped not to see food magically appear, but rather that the words alone would satisfy his hunger.

In Randall's estimation, this memory affirms little more than "that at three or four years old, he was taught to repeat his prayers," through which Jefferson "retained a familiarity with the Bible, with the prayers and collects of the noble Liturgy of the Church, and with its psalms and hymns, possessed by very few persons." Yet the account may also suggest that, for Jefferson, religion was by no means separate from worldly concerns, but rather something that might be instrumentalized to positive effect.[4]

Later in life Jefferson would recognize and write passionately about how religion might also be used for ill, but in the interim he learned that it could be merely dreary. His time spent boarding with the Scottish clergyman Reverend William Douglas from age nine to fourteen taught Jefferson that to be among the professionally religious did not necessarily make one particularly well suited to maintaining the health of the body or the expansion of the mind. He recalled his time there as filled with dinners of "mouldy pies," to which an empty plate and a prayer might have been preferred, and complained that his teacher was "a superficial Latinist, less instructed in Greek."[5] Even with such failings, however, Reverend Douglas managed to teach the young Jefferson the basics of both classical languages as well as French. Along with the King's English, these were the tongues he would later make use of when redacting the Gospels.

Though Jefferson's early education may have been wanting due to Douglas's deficiencies, it soon improved as the result of a silver lining in the emotional storm cloud brought by death of his father. Peter Jefferson's dying wish for his teenaged son was that he be thoroughly trained in the classics. The new tutor, Reverend James Maury, while likewise a man of the cloth, was also a man of books. Jefferson found in Maury's home a vast library that would serve as an early onset of the bibliophilia that would follow him happily through his days.

Despite this consistent and orthodox religious education, Jefferson admitted that he entertained doubts about the certain teachings of the church "from a very early part of my life." His particular qualms centered on the doctrine of the Trinity, which as he later wrote with a hint of ironic self-deprecation, he "never had sense enough to comprehend."[6]

This lack of comprehension, which is perhaps better understood as simply a lack of belief, seems to have been born out of the continuation of Jefferson's Anglican education. At the College of William and Mary, nearly all the faculty were Anglican divines, as Jefferson's early teachers had been. As such, they were required to affirm the Thirty-nine Articles of the Church of England, the very first of which was the concept that would later test his credulity: "Of Faith in the Holy Trinity." Moreover, the principal and masters of the college all signed an oath of affirmation to "avoid the danger of heresy, schism, and disloyalty."[7]

The sole outlier among this clergy-dominated faculty was a newly appointed professor of natural philosophy, William Small, who Jefferson would later describe as "a man profound in most of the useful branches of science, with a happy talent of communication, correct and gentlemanly manners, and an enlarged and liberal mind." It was from Small that Jefferson claimed to receive "my first views of science and the system of things in which we are placed"—his first views, in other words, of a universe moved by laws beyond traditional religious understanding.[8]

Small introduced his students to the works of John Locke, Francis Bacon, and Isaac Newton, whom for Jefferson quickly became a new trinity to replace the old. As Jefferson later wrote, "I consider them as the three greatest men that have ever lived, without any exception and as having laid the foundations of those superstructures which have been raised in the Physical & Moral sciences."[9]

Unlike the Trinity Jefferson found inscrutable in its dependence on mystery for its significance, the trinity he encountered under Small's tutelage proposed that the world was eminently knowable. All that these men had discovered of the universe and human society had been attained through reason—the application of the mind to observation and deduction. "From Bacon, Locke, and Newton," Gaustad wrote, "Jefferson learned to count, collect, explore, measure, observe, arrange, invent, and put his trust in the perceptions of the present rather than in the precedents of the distance past." Though eventually Jefferson focused his studies on law, the tenets of the Enlightenment composed his true education.[10]

* * *

Even with the new trinity's lessons, Jefferson might have remained comfortably within the "Anglican ambience" that challenged the authority of neither scripture nor crown, but other influences soon led him to question much of what he had previously taken for granted. In the "Literary Commonplace Book" Jefferson kept throughout the 1760s and which provides a précis of the reading that occupied years of his adulthood, the single most quoted source is Henry St. John. Also known as the first Viscount Bolingbroke, this somewhat scandalous thinker almost singlehandedly planted and cultivated a crisis of faith in the young Virginian.

Bolingbroke was an English member of parliament best known in Enlightenment circles for his critical writings on religion. As Samuel Johnson memorably summed up his incendiary rhetoric, which was not published until after his death, Bolingbroke "was a scoundrel, and a coward: a scoundrel for charging a blunderbuss against religion and morality; a coward, because he had not resolution to fire it off himself."[11]

Throughout his life Jefferson would recommend Bolingbroke's works "for the sake of the stile, which is declamatory and elegant." However, during the period in which his thoughts on religion were being transformed, Jefferson seems to have been drawn to the Viscount as much for his radical ideas as his facile pen.[12] For example, Bolingbroke wrote:

There are gross defects, and palpable falsehoods, in almost every page of the scriptures and the whole tenor of them is such as no man, who acknowledges a supreme, all-perfect Being, can believe it to be his word.[13]

Some of Bolingbroke's sharpest barbs against religion referred to the Hebrew scriptures, such as when he admitted "I cannot believe that the Pentateuch, and the other books of the Old Testament, were writ under a divine influence, and have any right to be called the word of God." But his critique did not shy away from the New Testament texts that would eventually cry out to Jefferson for redaction.[14] As Jefferson quoted with apparent approval:

When we meet with any record cited in history, we accept the historical proof, and content ourselves with it, of how many copies soever it may be the copy. But this proof would not be admitted in judicature. . . . nor any thing less than an attested copy of the record.[15]

In matters of history and religion, Bolingbroke argued and Jefferson concurred, while hearsay seemed to be sufficiently persuasive to many, the standards of present concerns were invariably higher. Bolingbroke wrote:

The application is obvious and if it be reasonable to take such a precaution in matters that concern private property, and wherein the sum of ten pounds may not be at stake, how much more reasonable is it to neglect no precaution, that can be taken to assure ourselves that we receive nothing for the word of God, which is not sufficiently attested to be so?[16]

At age 22, Jefferson copied by hand some ten thousand of Bolingbroke's words, among them judgments of the Gospels that were not quite as sharp tongued as those he directed at older texts. Nonetheless, Bolingbroke made light of the New Testament's merits when weighing them with the scales of the Enlightenment.

"It is not true that Christ revealed an entire body of ethics, proved to be the law of nature from principles of reason, and reaching all the duties of life," Bolingbroke wrote. Despite what some may claim, he argued, the Gospels did not provide any such code, but rather only gestured toward the need of its creation. "Moral obligations are occasionally recommended and commanded in it," he lamented, "but no where proved from principles of reason, and by clear deductions, unless allusions, parables, and comparisons, and promises, and threats, are to pass for such."[17]

Were one to attempt to piece together a reason-tested ethical guide from the New Testament, Bolingbroke suggested, one would find only "short sentences" scattered here and there throughout the Gospels. Anyone collecting them would note that "they would compose a very short as well as unconnected system of ethics."[18] It was beyond those short sentences, Bolingbroke ventured, where the true trouble with Christianity arose. Bolingbroke's dismantling of the biblical worldview ran from alpha to omega, the Garden to Golgotha, and Jefferson carefully copied it all in his own hand. One can only imagine the irreverent thrill of the boy who had once prayed to sate his hunger feverishly copying words so alien to the religious environment in which he was raised, making them his own by the physical act of writing.

In many instances, the young philosopher was undoubtedly trying blasphemy on for size, as when he noted that the foundational texts of his faith seemed incompatible with all virtue. For example, Jefferson copied from Bolingbroke:

> If the redemption be the main fundamental article of the Christian faith, sure I am that the account of the fall of man is the foundation of this fundamental article. And this account is, in all it's circumstances, absolutely irreconcilable to every idea we can frame of wisdom, justice, and goodness.[19]

Not even God was spared. "The supreme being," Bolingbroke noted, is introduced in scripture with such familiarity "and emploied so indecently" by taking walks in the cool air, making coats of skins, cursing both the serpent and humanity, that biblical divinity can hardly be taken seriously.[20]

Nor was the incarnation spared such unyielding logic. Jefferson further quoted Bolingbroke:

> God sent his only begotten son, who had not offended him, to be sacrificed by men, who had offended him, that he might expiate their sins, and satisfy his own anger. Surely our ideas of moral attributes will lead us to think that God would have been satisfied, more agreeably to his mercy and goodness, without any expiation, upon the repentance of the offenders, and more agreeably to his justice with any other expiation rather than this.... Can the innocence of the lamb of God, and the sufferings and ignominious death of Christ, be reconciled together?[21]

With the hindsight of history, it is impossible not to see Bolingbroke's exhortation to "receive nothing for the word of God which is not sufficiently attested to be so," along with his proposition that only "short sentences" might be gathered and collected from the New Testament into a new, albeit incomplete code of ethics as early signposts for a journey in which Jefferson's willingness to edit the Gospels would be the ultimate destination.

Yet, had Bolingbroke remained Jefferson's primary influence, he likely would not have bothered editing the text. In the Viscount's reading there was little worth saving in the whole of the Bible.

> Can any man now presume to say that the god of Moses, or the god of Paul, is this amiable being? The god of the first is partial, unjust, and cruel; delights in blood, commands assassinations, massacres, and even exterminations of people. The god of the second elects some of his creatures to salvation, and predestinates others to damnation, even in the womb of their mothers.[22]

A divine being such as that, and any book concerning its exploits, hardly seemed to Bolingbroke to be worth the effort of reconciling with reason. Jefferson's copying of this passage, along with all the others, suggests that, as a young man at least, he felt much the same way.

* * *

Jefferson's quiet rebellion against traditional Anglican belief did not make him an angry young man. Rather, it made him sympathetic to the notion of religious dissent at just the right time for this sympathy to have consequences for the nation soon to form. The stamp of his Enlightenment-influenced move away from the God of revelation and toward the God of nature can be seen in all the foundational documents which he had a hand in crafting. Both the Declaration of Independence's reference to "Nature's God" and the Virginia Statue of Religious Freedom's insistence that "civil rights have no dependence on our religious opinions" speak to the distance he had traveled, by 1776 and 1777 respectively, from the assumptions of revealed religion's role in the state. Of course, neither of these documents offered a scathing critique in the vein of Bolingbroke, but each acknowledged that ways of encountering and expressing religious ideas were, for Jefferson, no longer constrained by the Anglican ambience of his childhood.

Two dramatic statements of his religious convictions, made when Jefferson was fresh from the contest of establishing religious freedom in Virginia, reveal that by midlife the faith of his boyhood, if not entirely absent, had been scrupulously nudged aside by reason.

First published anonymously in Paris in 1785, *Notes on the State of Virginia* began as an assessment of the region of his youth written for a French diplomat and developed into a wide-ranging exploration of the requirements and responsibilities of a well-ordered society. In these *Notes*, Jefferson divided his thoughts on his home state—which was to him something of an America in miniature—into twenty-three categories, or queries, taking each in turn to create a kind of encyclopedia of a place, its past, and its potential. *Notes* also included Jefferson's most extensive articulation yet of his thinking on the subject of religion. Like his quotes from Bolingbroke twenty years before, his thoughts on the stifling nature of religious authority seem, when seen through the lens of the Jefferson Bible, a justification for the project he would undertake thirty-five years later:

Reason and free enquiry are the only effectual agents against error. Give a loose to them, they will support the true religion, by bringing every false one to their tribunal, to the test of their investigation. They are the natural enemies of error, and of error only. Had not the Roman government permitted free enquiry, Christianity could never have been introduced. Had not free enquiry been indulged, at the era of the reformation, the corruptions of Christianity could not have been purged away. If it be restrained now, the present corruptions will be protected, and new ones encouraged.[23]

Religion, for Jefferson, was a work in progress which could advance only if reason and free inquiry were left unrestrained. Where this naturally might lead he articulated soon after in a letter written to his nephew Peter Carr in 1787. In it, Jefferson encouraged the young man to do as he had done—to make "reason your only oracle"—but not to be disdainful of beliefs held by others simply because they are held by many: "Divest yourself of all bias in favour of novelty and singularity of opinion," he wrote. "Indulge them in any other subject rather than that of religion."[24]

At the same time, Jefferson stressed, one must not be so swayed by tradition or the crowd as to lose sight of one's individual responsibility to seek truth for oneself.

Shake off all the fears and servile prejudices under which weak minds are servilely crouched. Fix reason firmly in her seat, and call to her tribunal every fact, every opinion. Question with boldness even the existence of a god; because, if there be one, he must more approve the homage of reason, than that of blindfolded fear.

Jefferson then proceeded to call the Bible itself to reason's "tribunal." No matter the authority with which it was commonly viewed, Jefferson insisted, scripture should be regarded as any text might.

> Read the bible then, as you would read Livy or Tacitus. The facts which are within the ordinary course of nature you will believe on the authority of the writer, as you do those of the same kind in Livy and Tacitus. The testimony of the writer weighs in their favor in one scale, and their not being against the laws of nature does not weigh against them.

We see here Jefferson commending to paper for the first time the methodology that would lead him to cut the Bible's pages several decades hence.

> Those facts in the bible which contradict the laws of nature, must be examined with more care, and under a variety of faces. Here you must recur to the pretensions of the writer to inspiration from god. Examine upon what evidence his pretensions are founded, and whether that evidence is so strong as that it's falshood would be more improbable than a change of the laws of nature in the case he relates.

Within the intimate bounds of familial advice, Jefferson did not shy away from specifics. He pinpointed episodes in holy writ which he found strained belief.

> For example in the book of Joshua we are told the sun stood still several hours. Were we to read that fact in Livy or Tacitus we should class it with their showers of blood,

speaking of statues, beasts &c., but it is said that the writer of that book was inspired. Examine therefore candidly what evidence there is of his having been inspired. The pretension is entitled to your enquiry, because millions believe it. On the other hand you are Astronomer enough to know how contrary it is to the law of nature that a body revolving on it's axis, as the earth does, should have stopped, should not by that sudden stoppage have prostrated animals, trees, buildings, and should after a certain time have resumed it's revolution, and that without a second general prostration. Is this arrest of the earth's motion, or the evidence which affirms it, most within the law of probabilities?

Like Bolingbroke before him, Jefferson found it easiest to puncture the bubble of credulity surrounding the Hebrew scriptures, but for the sake of his nephew's learning he went further still.

You will next read the new testament. It is the history of a personage called Jesus. Keep in your eye the opposite pretensions. 1. Of those who say he was begotten by god, born of a virgin, suspended and reversed the laws of nature at will, and ascended bodily into heaven: and 2. of those who say he was a man, of illegitimate birth, of a benevolent heart, enthusiastic mind, who set out without pretensions to divinity, ended in believing them, and was punished capitally for sedition by being gibbeted according to the Roman law.

To take the proper measure of the New Testament and its claims, Jefferson advised, one must account for the assumptions behind both belief and its lack. He challenged the young man:

> Do not be frightened from this enquiry by any fear of it's consequences. If it ends in a belief that there is no god, you will find incitements to virtue in the comfort and pleasantness you feel in it's exercise, and the love of others which it will procure you. If you find reason to believe there is a god, a consciousness that you are acting under his eye, and that he approves you, will be a vast additional incitement. If that there be a future state, the hope of a happy existence in that increases the appetite to deserve it; if that Jesus was also a god, you will be comforted by a belief of his aid and love.

Over all, Jefferson insisted that his young nephew take nothing for granted, not the words of scripture, not the reliability of its authors, and not the centuries of tradition that had shored up each.

> In fine, I repeat that you must lay aside all prejudice on both sides, and neither believe nor reject any thing because any other person, or description of persons have rejected or believed it. Your own reason is the only oracle given you by heaven, and you are answerable not for the rightness but uprightness of the decision.

In his letter to Peter Carr, Jefferson comes off as one who could take or leave both testaments of the Bible. He could see the social good in scripture, but also the reasons why one might turn away from some of its teachings. The challenge faced by everyone who encounters such a text, he suggested, was in the responsibility to make a choice about how it should be read, weighing its various elements with the scales of reason. In other words, by the late 1780s Jefferson had begun to develop the methodology with which he would remake the Gospels, but he still needed the inspiration to do so.

Making the Cut

When the dissenting English clergyman Joseph Priestley arrived in the young United States, his flight from religious persecution inspired Jefferson to compare the theologian, philosopher, and chemist to another famous "first observer of marvelous things": Galileo Galilei.[1]

"Antagonists think they have quenched his opinions by sending him to America," Jefferson remarked of Priestley and the mob that burned down his English home in 1791, "just as the Pope imagined when he shut up Galileo in prison that he had compelled the world to stand still."[2]

In the realm of science, Priestley is best known as the man who discovered oxygen by isolating various gases in airtight glass vessels. In the realm of American religion and politics, his greatest contribution may have been serving as another significant influence on Jefferson's religious views. Along with Bolingbroke, Priestley was a godfather of the Jefferson Bible. In fact, had Jefferson had his way, it might have been Priestley who wielded the blade instead of himself.

Jefferson soon would consider the minister a trusted confidant, but he knew him first only by reputation. When compiling a list of recommended reading for the son of a friend early in the 1770s, in the short category on religion Jefferson had suggested Priestley's book *A History of the Corruptions of Christianity*, along with the Bible. As Jefferson later owned a 1793 edition of the former, it is likely he returned to the text around the time its author settled in Pennsylvania in 1794. Soon thereafter, the Unitarian scientist arguably took the place of Bolingbroke as the primary influence on Jefferson's understanding of religion.

The "plain doctrine of the Scriptures," Priestley wrote, was "a doctrine . . . consonant to reason and the ancient prophecies." And yet, to his consternation:

> Christians have at length come to believe what they do not pretend to have any conception of, and than which it is not possible to frame a more express contradiction. For, while they consider Christ as the supreme, eternal God, the maker of heaven and earth, and of all things visible and invisible, they moreover acknowledge the Father and the Holy Spirit to be equally God in the same exalted sense, all three equal in power and glory, and yet all three constituting no more than one God.[3]

For Priestley, this paradox was not something to accept with a shrugging faith, but to be investigated. "To a person the least interested in the inquiry," he wrote, "it must appear an object of curiosity to trace by what means, and by what steps, so great a change has taken place."[4]

The notion that it was the changes that had taken place in Christianity, rather than Christianity itself, that had conditioned his youthful crisis of faith seems to have come as a revelation to Jefferson, and a relief. In particular, Jefferson found in Priestley the suggestion that the figure of Jesus, who in the Anglican ambience of Jefferson's boyhood had been inseparable from the traditions of the church, had been most badly served by it. According to Priestley:

> Jesus Christ, whose history answers to the description given of the Messiah by the prophets, made no other pretensions; referring all his extraordinary power to God, his Father, who, he expressly says, spake and acted by him, and who raised him from the dead: and it is most evident that the apostles, and all those who conversed with our Lord before and after his resurrection, considered him in no other light than simply as "a man approved of God, by wonders and signs which God did by him." (Acts ii:22)[5]

From Priestley, Jefferson also came to see that there were layers of material in the Gospel accounts of the life and work of Jesus, and that through a careful reading one could catch glimpses of the truth. In Jefferson's interpretation of Priestley's assessment, that truth was that the man who had started it all was only a man.

> Nothing can be alleged from the New Testament in favor of any higher nature of Christ except a few passages interpreted without any regard to the context, or the modes of speech and opinions of the times in which the books were written, and in such a manner, in other respects, as would authorize our proving any doctrine whatever from them.[6]

In actuality, Priestley was far more willing than Jefferson came to be to accept the divinity of Christ and the authority of scripture. Nonetheless, in this exiled Unitarian, Jefferson believed he had found a man who had reconciled the faith with which he had been raised and the reason to which he aspired.

The two men met in 1797 in Philadelphia, where Priestley had been occupied giving public lectures. Though he had been chased out of England as a dissenter by those with more orthodox religious views, in America he had come to see himself as a defender of the faith. Around this time he wrote:

> Considering my situation in this country, I may almost say with the apostle, I am set for the defence of the gospel, for nobody else seems disposed to do it. Indeed, but few, I believe, are at all qualified for it. They can bawl out against me as a heretic loud enough, but they have nothing to say to the common enemy, so that I have to look two ways at the same time.[7]

That common enemy, of orthodox ministers and dissenters alike, was unbelief—an enemy Priestley feared may have been present even when he first met Jefferson. "Mr. Jefferson has been here, and I have seen a good deal of him," Priestley wrote to his fellow Unitarian minister Thomas Belsham in England. "He came to hear me, and I hope he is not an unbeliever, as he has been represented."[8]

By the time of their meeting, the notion that Jefferson was an infidel, an atheist, or worse was a common note struck by his political rivals. His advocacy against the establishment of his own Anglican church, though pursued in the defense of religious liberty, was interpreted by many as a general antipathy toward religion. If Jefferson had his way, his critics warned, churches would become "temples of reason" and "the Bible cast into a Bonfire."[9]

That such warnings were amplified mainly by his Federalist foes did not lessen their efficacy or persistence, as Priestley's earliest concerns about Jefferson attest. The minister may have even seen the possibility that the then-vice president was an "unbeliever" as a challenge. "The progress of infidelity here is very great," Priestley wrote, "though in some instances I have been of some use in stopping it."[10]

It's possible that Priestley played a role in stopping such tendencies in Jefferson. His approach to Christianity offered Jefferson an alternative to both Bolingbroke's strident dismissals and deistic indifference to Christian moral teachings which Jefferson regarded as useful no matter their connection to beliefs he could not affirm.

Soon after their meeting, with Priestley finally convinced that Jefferson was not an enemy of the faithful, the two struck up an ongoing correspondence that lasted through the next several years and continued unabated when Jefferson ascended to the White House in the Election of 1800. It was from there that Jefferson wrote in 1803 to thank Priestley for sending his latest book, a comparison of the teachings of Jesus and Socrates. Jefferson was so taken by the book he ventured to share that he had long considered something similar: a comparison of "the most remarkable of the ancient philosophers," including not just Socrates, but Pythagoras, Epicurus, Epictetus, Cicero, and Seneca, with "the life, character, & doctrines of Jesus."[11]

To do him [Jesus] justice, it would be necessary to remark the disadvantages his doctrines have to encounter, not having been committed to writing by himself, but by the most unlettered of men, by memory, long after they had heard them from him; when much was forgotten, much misunderstood, & presented in very paradoxical shapes. . . . His character & doctrines have received still greater injury from those who pretend to be his special disciples, and who have disfigured and sophisticated his actions & precepts.

As Jefferson saw it, any fair comparison between Jesus and other moral teachers must thus account for, or simply set aside, those elements which had come to obscure Jesus's original teachings. He continued:

Yet such are the fragments remaining as to shew a master workman, and that his system of morality was the most benevolent & sublime probably that has been ever taught; and eminently more perfect than those of any of the ancient philosophers.

Jefferson went so far as to enclose for Priestley an outline of the plan he hoped to undertake, but lamented:

I have not the time, & still less the information which the subject needs. It will therefore rest with me in contemplation only. You are the person who of all others would do it best, and most promptly. You have all the materials at hand, and you put together with ease. I wish you could be induced to extend your late work to the whole subject.

Jefferson's enthusiasm for this idea was such that two weeks later he wrote another letter, explaining his plans to another friend, Dr. Benjamin Rush.

While on the road, and unoccupied otherwise, [I began] to arrange in my mind a Syllabus, or Outline, of such an

Estimate of the comparative merits of Christianity, as I wished to see executed, by some one of more leisure and information for the task than myself.[12]

This "Syllabus," as he continued to call it throughout his life, became for Jefferson both a shibboleth and a millstone.

In confiding it to you, I know it will not be exposed to the malignant perversions of those who make every word from me a text for new misrepresentations & calumnies.

Eight months later, it was still on Jefferson's mind. He wrote again to Priestley with addenda to his suggestion that the latter take on the project which naturally the President of the United States might not have time to entertain.

I think you cannot avoid giving, as preliminary to the comparison, a digest of his moral doctrines, extracted in his own words from the Evangelists, and leaving out everything relative to his personal history and character. It would be short and precious.

With a view to do this for my own satisfaction, I had sent to Philadelphia to get two testaments (Greek) of the same edition, and two English, with a design to cut out the morsels of morality, and paste them on the leaves of a book. . . . But I shall now get the thing done by better hands.[7]

Whether Priestley was up to the challenge, we will never know. He died before receiving Jefferson's last letter to him, and so it fell to Jefferson to follow through on his designs with the New Testament editions he had recently purchased. The result was not the Jefferson Bible, but rather something of a proof of concept: a 46-page work he called *The Philosophy of Jesus*, his first collection of edited Gospel verses. Nearly a decade later, Jefferson described the completion of this work in a letter to John Adams.

> In extracting the pure principles which he taught, we should have to strip off the artificial vestments in which they have been muffled by priests, who have travestied them into various forms . . . We must reduce our volume to the simple evangelists, select, even from them, the very words only of Jesus, paring off the Amphibologisms into which they have been led by forgetting often, or not understanding, what had fallen from him, by giving their own misconceptions as his dicta, and expressing unintelligibly for others what they had not understood themselves. There will be found remaining the most sublime and benevolent code of morals which has ever been offered to man.[13]

The verbs Jefferson chose here speak volumes: "extracting"; "strip"; "reduce"; "paring." Each speaks as a carver would of stone, removing raw material until an elegant form emerges from a block of wood or stone. Going further, he refined the idea so that its echoes were not just artistic but surgical, as if this was an act undertaken to save a life. Jefferson confided to Adams:

> I have performed this operation for my own use by cutting verse by verse out of the printed book, and arranging the matter which is evidently his, and which is as easily distinguishable as diamonds in a dunghill. The result is an 8vo of 46 pages of pure and unsophisticated doctrines,

such as were professed & acted on by the <u>unlettered</u> apostles, the Apostolic fathers, and the Christians of the 1st century.

The *Philosophy of Jesus* has unfortunately been lost to history, but even in its absence it has served to shape impressions of the book that would follow it. The full title given the initial effort was *The Philosophy of Jesus of Nazareth: extracted from the account of his life and doctrines as given by Matthew, Mark, Luke, & John. Being an abridgement of the New Testament for the use of the Indians unembarrassed with matters of fact or faith beyond the level of their comprehensions.*

The suggestion that this book was prepared for "use of the Indians" presents something of a puzzle. While it has been taken at face value as long as the full title of the project has been known, it is not entirely certain that this was Jefferson's intention. In the presentation of a scholarly recreation of the *Philosophy of Jesus* which appears in *Jefferson's Extracts from the Gospels*, Dickinson Adams persuasively made the case, later affirmed by Monticello's *Thomas Jefferson Encyclopedia*, that this subtitle was an "intentionally ironic" jab at the Federalists critics who had questioned Jefferson's allegience to Christianity. "The 'Indians' Jefferson had in mind were not the aboriginal inhabitants of North America," Adams argued. "They were, rather, the Federalists and their clerical allies, whose political and religious obscurantism . . . endangered the stability of the republic and needed to be reformed by a return to the simple, uncorrupted morality of Jesus." [14]

Given that nowhere in his correspondence did Jefferson propose his biblical abridgement was being done for the sake of Native Americans, it seems plausible that in claiming to make the most important moral lessons of the Gospels impossible to miss even by those "unembarrassed with matters of fact or faith beyond the level of their comprehensions," he may have been having a private laugh at his opponents' expense.

Ten years after making this rough draft of the Jefferson Bible, his undiminished enthusiasm for the project in his correspondence with John Adams suggests that Jefferson may soon have turned to the expanded enterprise of adding other versions of the text. Yet in the year following his last mention of the project to Adams, the world intervened.

* * *

In early September 1814, Jefferson read of the destruction recently wrought in Washington in a Richmond newspaper. As a final act of insult and injury during the waning days of the War of 1812, the British had burned much of the capital—including, to any bibliophile's horror, the Congressional Library.

Five years out of office and retired to Monticello, Jefferson decided to act. "I learn from the newspapers that the vandalism of our enemy has triumphed at Washington over science as well as the arts," he wrote in a letter submitted to members of Congress. Suspecting they would like to rebuild the collection but might find it difficult during wartime, he proposed the country buy his own carefully curated personal library as a replacement.

When Jefferson first offered to make his books available, the most vexing matter to some critics was the expense. At a price of $23,950 for 6,487 books (in today's dollars, an average cost of more than fifty dollars each), a price determined by a Georgetown bookseller, the library was no bargain. For months the debate about the purchase dragged on in the press and through a vote in the Senate; however, this concern was often eclipsed by another: the supposedly "atheistical" character of the former president's book collection.

Far from strictly atheist, Jefferson's books included texts from a number of religious traditions. He owned a score of Bibles, a Quran, a history of "heathen gods," and works by Deist philosophers—and that was precisely the problem. Such heterodox titles reflected his opinion that religion should be a personal affair, guided by curiosity and reason.

Though only dozens of the more than six thousand books dealt with religion, they were seen by some as a window into a dangerously pluralistic worldview. Faced with restocking the contents of the Congressional Library, opponents of heterodoxy were horrified by the notion that Jefferson's famously eclectic opinions would soon form the core of a national storehouse of knowledge.

Within weeks of Jefferson writing his letter, the national press began to cover his offer to sell his books as if it was a scandal. The *Federal Republican* sarcastically supposed that the "Library of the Sage of Monticello" contained "a plentiful stock of the works of Tom Paine, Rousseau, Voltaire, Condorcet," all bywords for unbelief in the public imagination.[15] An article first published in Connecticut but then republished throughout the states took issue with the sheer variety of the collection, with his eclectic religious interests becoming the crux of the issue:

> We understand that Mr. Jefferson's *invaluable* collection of Books contains, among others, more than 40

Romances in French, Spanish, and Italian—12 different treatises on music—playing the violin, fingering the harp, &c.... We have no doubt that Mr. Jefferson has not only *some*, but *an extensive 'knowledge of the bibliography of these subjects,'* particularly infidelity and architecture. With respect to the latter, it is said he is so great an adept as to posses a complete assortment of Joiner's tools, and with regard to the former, he is considered still more accomplished—being a master-workman.[16]

As Jefferson's longtime antagonists at the *Federal Republican* stated most plainly, the opposition feared that, if the former president's books were accepted, the Congressional Library would be filled "with productions of atheistical, irreligious, and immoral character."[17]

By January 26, 1815, when the bill allowing purchase of the library came up for a vote in the House, Jefferson's critics had stirred themselves into a witch hunt. The Federalist representative Cyrus King of Massachusetts argued that the character of the man who assembled the library, and the place where he had acquired much of it—France—was evidence enough that the collection contained "many books of irreligious and immoral tendency." Attempting to prevent "a general dissemination of this infidel philosophy," King declared that the books would be better off burned than bought with public funds.[18]

Other members of Congress found this talk of book burning too much to take. Representative James Fisk of Vermont, a Democratic-Republican like Jefferson, reminded his fellow congressmen that King came from a state once known for hanging witches, and wondered whether that practice might also be reintroduced. Representative Robert Wright of Maryland accused King of wanting to start an Inquisition. To this charge, King replied that he had no such intention—at least not while his party was in the minority.[19]

Even then, party politics ruled the day. With the Democratic-Republicans holding a majority in both houses, King's Federalists saw the purchase of the library as an abuse of power directly enriching a political rival. As extreme as that position might seem from the distance of centuries, forty-seven percent of the House agreed with King. In the end, the bill passed, but barely. President James Madison approved the act of Congress purchasing Jefferson's library on January 30, 1815, and word reached Monticello in early February. By May of that year, ten wagons had hauled the books to the national capital, providing a model for the enormously wide-ranging collection the Library of Congress would become.

Despite coming under scathing personal attack, Jefferson sat out the battle over his library's supposedly heretical content. He was, after all, retired from public life by then, and less willing, or able, as he grew older to engage with critics and political rivals as he once had. Moreover, he had surely grown tired of fighting this particular battle again and again.

Jefferson was no stranger to religious conflict. The presidential election of 1800 had been in many ways a referendum on his faith—or lack thereof, according to his detractors. Allies of his opponent in the contest, the incumbent John Adams, had not shied away from exploiting the widespread suspicion of Jefferson's beliefs for their own benefit.

As one slogan of the time put it, the choice between the sitting president and his challenger was clear: "God and a religious president, or Jefferson and no god."[20] Jefferson was no more popular in the pulpits, where one preacher warned that under Jefferson, "Murder, robbery, rape, adultery, and incest will be openly taught and practiced, the air will be rent with the cries of the distressed, the soil will be soaked with blood, and the nation black with crimes."[21]

As with his library, the problem Jefferson presented was not atheism per se, but that belief which, in the intervening centuries, has fully lost its capacity to strike fear in Christian hearts: deism. To many orthodox Christians in the early nineteenth century, to refer to the divine as "nature's God," as deists did, was as good as saying there was no god at all. God, to those Christians, was simply and unquestionably the divinity made manifest in the revelation of the Gospels and in the person of Jesus Christ. Appeals to a god of nature that was somehow independent of salvation history were regarded as theological doubletalk. As with the anti-Jefferson slogan mentioned previously, one was either with God or against God, and deists were certainly regarded as against, no matter the vague philosophical defense they might make.

Though Jefferson was somewhat insulated at Monticello, the echoes of the arguments in Washington and the press over his library found him even there. In December 1814, a letter arrived that warned Jefferson of the consequences if he should follow through on plans to expand his earlier experiment in biblical redaction.

The Reverend Charles Clay was a Virginia minister for whom, in 1779, Jefferson wrote a testimonial praising his "deportment" and "attention to parochial duties." [22] On December 20, 1814, Clay wrote to Jefferson in a state of quiet alarm. He made no mention of the debate over Jefferson's alleged atheism, but given the attention it was then receiving, it cannot have been far from his mind.

> Reflecting on an expression of yours Relative to an Idea Sometimes entertained by you of Compresing the Moral doctrines taught by Jesus of Nazareth in the Gospels, I cannot help entertaining doubts & fears for the final issue, how it may effect your future character & Reputation on the page of history as a Patriot, legislator & sound Philosopher.[23]

Clay allowed that Jefferson's notion of presenting the teachings of Jesus "divested of all other Matters into a small and Regular system of the purest morality ever taught to Mankind" would be "laudable" and his intentions "meritorious." But he cautioned that the work would necessarily be "delicate."

> Should you be induced to permit yourself to Send forth Such a piece to the public, lest they might not sufficiently appreciate your good intentions, but ascribe it to Views as inimical to the christian Religion in particular, & eventually to all Religion from divine Authority,— which I am persuaded you Can have no intention of doing.

The reverend then reminded his old friend that, no matter "its excesses, extravagances, or abusives," it was better for the world to have even a corrupted Christianity than no Christianity at all. Without the divine sanction it provided, Clay

warned, it was likely "no System of morality however pure it
might be . . . would have sufficient weight on Vulgar minds
to ensure an Observance internal and external."

Yet Clay's true concern was not for the vulgar minds that
might fall into immorality, but rather for Jefferson himself.

> My fears are, that should your performance not exactly
> meet the approbation of the public, both now & here-
> after, that your Name will be degraded from the Vener-
> able Council of true, genuine, Useful Philosophy;
> & Condemned to be Ranked with the wild Sophisters
> of Jacobinism the Theosophies of Masonry, With
> Martinists, Swedenborgers, & Rosecrusians, with the
> Epopts & Magi of Illuminism &c. which Phantastic
> kind of beings, future Historians will most assuredly
> denominate by Some opprobious epithet, as the mani-
> acs of Philosophy.

Worst of all, if it became known that Jefferson had dared
compress scripture, the Federalists who were even then de-
bating the contents of his library would surely say even
worse about the contents of his soul.

> And it certainly may be expected that the whole of your
> numerous Enimies in the Northern & eastern parts of
> the U.S. with all their Friends, Disciples, followers & as-
> sociates through out America; (& who it must be Con-
> fessed possess Considerable influence in the public edu-
> cation & Consequently in forming the Opinion of the
> Rising generation) should the performance not exactly
> Coincide with their Ideas & meet their entire approba-
> tion, even in the minutiæ of diction (which it is highly

probable it would not) they would greedily Seize the Occasion, & Raise the hue & Cry after you through the world, & all the Canaille of America & Europe would be found barking at your heels!

Jefferson sent his response just as the purchase of his library was being approved, a day before the bill was signed into law by his old friend James Madison. He assured Reverend Clay that the concerns he raised were "founded on a misconception":

Of publishing a book on religion, my dear Sir, I never had an idea. I should as soon think of writing for the reformation of Bedlam, as of the world of religious sects. Of these there must be at least ten thousand, every individual of every one of which believes all are wrong but his own. To undertake to bring them all right, would be like undertaking, single handed, to fell the forests of America.

. . .

Probably you have heard me say I had taken the four evangelists, had cut out from them every text they had recorded of the moral precepts of Jesus, and arranged them in a certain order, and altho' they appeared but as fragments, yet fragments of the most sublime edifice of morality which had ever been exhibited to man. this I have probably mentioned to you, because it is true; and the idea of it's publication may have suggested itself as an inference of your own mind.[24]

Despite his downplaying of the significance of his project to the nervous Rev. Clay, at other times, Jefferson hinted that he was aware of its radical implications, as in 1816 when he confided to Charles Thompson that he had "made a wee little book . . . which I call the *Philosophy of Jesus*":

> It is a paradigma of his doctrines, made by cutting the texts out of the book, and arranging them on the pages of a blank book, in a certain order of time or subject. A more beautiful or precious morsel of ethics I have never seen; it is document in proof that I am a real Christian, that is to say, a disciple of the doctrines of Jesus, very different from the Platonists, who call <u>me</u> infidel, and themselves Christians and preachers of the gospel, while they draw all their characteristic dogmas from what it's Author never said nor saw. They have compounded from the heathen mysteries a system beyond the comprehension of man, of which the great reformer of the vicious ethics and deism of the Jews, were he to return on earth, would not recognise one feature. If I had time I would add to my little book the Greek, Latin and French texts, in columns side by side.[25]

Given the debate surrounding Jefferson's religious proclivities that had only recently raged in the press and the capital, one can read this letter as both defense and rebuke. First, it was an insistence that he was no infidel at all, but a true Christian. Yet simultaneously Jefferson could not resist redefining what Christian should mean, in contradistinction to all those who practiced something they called Christianity but was, in his view, a different creed altogether. While Jefferson insisted that there would be no publication, the temptation remained to go even further down the path he had started—toward producing not just a compressed version of the Gospels, but one that was wholly remade.

For more than a decade before he finally made his first incisions, Jefferson had on hand the materials necessary to create the book he came to call *The Life and Morals of Jesus of Nazareth.* He had purchased two copies of a Greek-Latin New Testament in 1804, two copies of a French edition of *le Nouveau testament* in January 1805, and two new English editions later that year. As he acquired these books while in Washington, they likely sat for several years on a White House bookshelf in the room Jefferson called his cabinet, which according to a contemporary account, "he had arranged according to his own taste and convenience." The spacious room included not only walls filled with maps, globes, charts, and books, but also a collection of carpentry and gardening tools, "the use of which he derived much amusement."[26] This was likely the room where the *Philosophy of Jesus* was created, but if the juxtaposition of saws and shears to his books put him in mind of further redaction projects involving his recently acquired Bibles, he left no record of these thoughts.

When Jefferson returned to Monticello in 1809, the six books that together would become the Jefferson Bible went with him. There they sat through a decade that saw a new war on American shores, and new controversies surrounding the former president and his religious convictions. Through all of this, perhaps what he lacked was the time for a so purely personal endeavor, or else Jefferson was simply waiting until he had been out of public life long enough that he could pursue his idea of editing the Gospels in peace.

Jefferson's final incentive seems to have come from one of his oldest friends. Though just sixteen years his junior, William Short was regarded by Jefferson as an "adoptive son." He had served as secretary during the latter's time as Minister to France in the 1780s, and after that enjoyed a long career as a diplomat and financier. Short had, Jefferson once observed, "a peculiar talent for prying into facts" and in a series of letters exchanged throughout 1819 and 1820 he did precisely that regarding his mentor's enduring interest in what a careful reading of the Bible might reveal.[27]

Jefferson had shared some of his reflections along these lines, but indicated that his decision to devote himself to "the delights of classical reading and of mathematical truths" would preclude his giving them further attention. To this, Short wrote back in apparent distress: "I see with real pain that you have no intention of continuing the abstract from the Evangelists which you begun at Washington." Reminding him of his often-stated belief that the true teachings of Jesus could be readily separated from distortions wrought over time, Short sought to persuade Jefferson of the importance of such an effort.[28]

> You observe that what is genuine is easily distinguished from the rubbish in which it is buried—if so, it is an irresistible reason for your continuing the work—for others, it would seem, have not found it thus distinguishable—& I fear I should be of the number if I were to undertake this study. It would cost you but little trouble on a fair edition of this book, if you would by mere lines mark off what appeared to you thus manifestly genuine.

Writing in response in April 1820, Jefferson sent Short the outline of Gospel verses he had compiled for Benjamin Rush fifteen years before, along with a further insistence that this would be his final word on the matter. The possibility of being misunderstood was simply too great. Yet in articulating why this was likely to be the extent of his further effort on the subject, Jefferson began to articulate the ways in which his thinking about the Gospels and their central figure had continued to develop.

While this Syllabus is meant to place the character of Jesus in it's true and high light, as no imposter himself, but a great Reformer of the Hebrew code of religion, it is not to be understood that I am with him in all his doctrines. I am a Materialist; he takes the side of spiritualism: he preaches the efficacy of repentance towards forgiveness of sin, I require a counterpoise of good works to redeem it.[29]

Despite these differences, there remained something singular and important about Jesus for Jefferson.

It is the innocence of his character, the purity & sublimity of his moral precepts, the eloquence of his inculcations, the beauty of the apologues in which he conveys them, that I so much admire; sometimes indeed needing indulgence to Eastern hyperbolism.

This respect, Jefferson explained, was the source of his enduring discomfort with the accounts of the life and ministry of Jesus that had been passed down by centuries of religious tradition.

Among the sayings & discourses imputed to him by his biographers, I find many passages of fine imagination, correct morality, and of the most lovely benevolence; and others again of so much ignorance, so much absurdity, so much untruth; charlatanism, and imposture, as to pronounce it impossible that such contradictions should have proceeded from the same being. I separate therefore the gold from the dross; restore to him the former, & leave the latter to the stupidity of some, and roguery of others of his disciples.

These palpable interpolations and falsifications of his doctrines led me to try to sift them apart. I found the work obvious and easy, and that his part composed the most beautiful morsel of morality which has been given to us by man. the Syllabus is therefore of <u>his</u> doctrines, not <u>all</u> of <u>mine</u>. I read them as I do those of other ancient and modern moralists, with a mixture of approbation and dissent.

Here, for the first time, Jefferson described the work of crafting *The Life and Morals of Jesus of Nazareth* not as something he hoped to do, but rather a task in which he seems to have been currently engaged.

Five months later, on August 20, 1820, Jefferson wrote Short again, offering what he called a "supplement" to his April letter. In it, Jefferson argued that reading the Bible should be no different from reading any text from history. If a historian writes of events in such a way that they "coincide with our experience of the order of nature, we credit them on their word, and place their narrations among the records of credible history," Jefferson wrote. If, on the other hand, a historian describes things that simply could never be—"when they tell us of calves speaking, of statues sweating blood, and other things against the course of nature"—their word should be rejected as mere stories, the trickery of a charlatan, or the ramblings of a fool.[30]

> This free exercise of reason is all I ask for the vindication of the character of Jesus. We find in the writings of his biographers matter of two distinct descriptions. First a ground work of vulgar ignorance, of things impossible, of superstitions, fanaticisms, & fabrications. Intermixed with these again are sublime ideas of the supreme being, aphorisms and precepts of the purest morality & benevolence, sanctioned by a life of humility, innocence, and simplicity of manners, neglect of riches, absence of worldly ambition & honors, with an eloquence and persuasiveness which have not been surpassed. These could not be inventions of the grovelling authors who relate them. They are far beyond the powers of their feeble minds. They shew that there was a character, the subject of their history, whose splendid conceptions were above all suspicion of being interpolations from their hands.

Faced with such an obvious difference of tone and subject, Jefferson argued:

> can we be at a loss in separating such materials, & ascribing each to it's genuine author? The difference is obvious to the eye and to the understanding, and we may read; as we run, to each his part.

In this letter, though Jefferson did not state plainly that he had finally finished what he had so long in mind, he did indicate that the work was no longer in the future or ongoing, but accomplished.

And I will venture to affirm that he who, as I have done, will undertake to winnow this grain from it's chaff, will find it not to require a moment's consideration; the parts fall asunder of themselves as would those of an image of metal & clay.

All told, a half century passed between Jefferson's first encounter, in the writings of Bolingbroke, with the intellectual dismantling of scripture and the literal dismantling of the New Testament he would undertake to fashion *The Life and Morals of Jesus of Nazareth.* A quarter century passed between Jefferson's reading of Priestley's historical effort to salvage Christianity from its corruptions and his textual effort to do the same.

The Jefferson Bible was, in this sense at least, a life's work. Throughout one of the most consequential lifetimes in American history, during revolution, the crafting of new laws, and the building of a new nation, the notion at the heart of the book nagged at Jefferson. In its execution he presented a surprising manifestation of a quintessentially American idea: that existing materials might be reshaped into something new.

The Quest for the Jeffersonian Jesus

On the dedication page to their controversial volume *The Five Gospels: The Search for the Authentic Words of Jesus,* the biblical scholars Robert Funk and Roy Hoover did not choose to honor a family member or a mentor, but rather a man not usually associated with biblical criticism: "Thomas Jefferson, who took scissors and paste to the gospels."[1]

Funk and Hoover, along with more than a hundred other scholars who together made up an international group known as the Jesus Seminar, had spent the preceding decade reevaluating some 1,500 sayings attributed to Jesus in the New Testament and the non-canonical Gospel of Thomas. By voting with colored beads dropped into a box on the likelihood that a given phrase had actually passed Jesus's lips, this group produced a color-coded volume in which:

> only those sayings that appear in red type are considered by the Seminar to be close to what Jesus actually said; the words in pink less certainly originated with Jesus; the words in gray are not his, though they contain ideas that are close to his own; the sayings that appear in black have

been embellished or created by his followers, or borrowed from common lore.[2]

Through this rubric, the Jesus Seminar argued that no more than twenty percent of the words long believed to be Jesus's own were authentic.

The Jesus Seminar's choice of Jefferson as something of a patron saint of this project might have puzzled some, but their stated aims so resonated with his own that he likely would have applauded the effort, even while appreciating its risks. As Funk said of the goals of the Jesus Seminar at the opening of their first meeting in 1985:

> We are going to inquire simply, rigorously after the voice of Jesus, after what he really said. In this process, we will be asking a question that borders the sacred, that even abuts blasphemy, for many in our society. As a consequence, the course we shall follow may prove hazardous. We may well provoke hostility . . .
>
> Our basic plan is simple. We intend to examine every fragment of the traditions attached to the name of Jesus in order to determine what he really said—not his literal words, perhaps, but the substance and style of his utterances. We are in quest of his *voice*, insofar as it can be distinguished from many other voices also preserved in the tradition.[3]

Much as Jefferson had sifted wheat from chaff, the Jesus Seminar judged every word attributed to Jesus and sorted them into four piles, allowing for greater nuance and ambiguity than the unforgiving blade unsheathed at Monticello in 1820. Unlike Jefferson, of course, the Jesus Seminar believed this work of sifting should be done not merely for one's own benefit but the greater good, and so must be done in the open. As Funk said, speaking for the group:

> We are going to carry out our work in full public view. We will insist on the public disclosure of our work and, insofar as it lies within our power, we shall see to it that the public is informed of our judgments.[4]

Thanks to the Jesus Seminar's apparent zeal for its work to receive as much attention as possible, at least one critic suggested that P.T. Barnum would have been a fitting choice to share the dedication page of *The Five Gospels* with Jefferson.[5] Yet it was Jefferson far more than Funk et al. who carried out his project with a showman's swagger.

Despite the long delay between conception and completion, when Jefferson finally set about extracting the passages to be included in his radically abridged Gospel, it seems he did so with the utmost assurance. While the Jesus Seminar described its voting process as "glacially slow, painful, and usually indecisive,"[6] Jefferson knew the type of Jesus he hoped to present, and was able, or so he boasted, to easily differentiate the passages contributing to this portrait from those that might distract from it.

For all his concern about contradictions in the Bible, however, Jefferson's efforts at reconstructing Jesus brought problems all their own. Emphatically not both God and man, Jefferson's Jesus somehow seems to be neither, as this chapter will consider.

If Jefferson's creation did not fully measure up to his confidence, he may perhaps be forgiven. Jefferson did not have the benefit of more recent efforts to separate the "authentic" words of Jesus from subsequent accretions. *The Life and Morals of Jesus of Nazareth* predates the first meetings of the Jesus Seminar by one hundred and sixty-five years. So too, Jefferson's first pass at the project—1804's *The Philosophy of Jesus*—predated by a century Albert Schweitzer's coining of the term the "quest for the historical Jesus," in the book by the same name, and the great flowering of interest in the "life of Christ" generally.

Yet Jefferson shared inspiration with some of the earliest instigators of this quest. Perhaps the first, Hermann Samuel Reimarus, died while the young Virginian law student was deep in his reading of Bolingbroke. The German Deist philosopher's posthumously published essay "The Aims of Jesus and His Disciples" made the novel proposal that there were indeed two sets of "aims" to be found in the New Testament—those of Jesus himself and those of the men who called themselves his followers. First printed in 1778, the essay appeared only in German for a century, but in it can be found many notes resonant with Jefferson's methodology of distinguishing between multiple levels of intention and discourse in the Gospels. As Reimarus wrote:

> We are justified in drawing an absolute distinction between the teaching of the Apostles in their writings and what Jesus Himself in His own lifetime proclaimed and taught.[7]

At times, the distinctions Reimarus made seem nearly Jeffersonian in their insistence on comparing the events of scripture with the laws of nature. "No miracle would prove that two and two make five, or that a circle has four angles," he wrote, "and no miracles, however numerous, could remove a contradiction which lies on the surface of the teachings and records of Christianity."[8]

According to Schweitzer, the conclusions drawn by Reimarus reveal that the difference between his understanding of Jesus and Jefferson's own could not be greater. For Reimarus, "what belongs to the preaching of Jesus is clearly to be recognised. It is contained in two phrases of identical meaning, 'Repent, and believe the Gospel,' or, as it is put elsewhere, 'Repent, for the Kingdom of Heaven is at hand.'"[9]

Christ was not an enlightened sage or a timeless moral exemplar offering wisdom for the ages, but a man of his era who could offer only teachings for his time and his people. For Reimarus, it was clear that Jesus was a prophet preaching the end of an existing order in a distinctly Jewish mode—in other words, "that Jesus had not the slightest intention of doing away with the Jewish religion and putting another in its place."[10] The mission of Reimarus's Jesus was to end the political oppression of Jews living under Roman rule. When this failed to happen, and Jesus instead died on the cross, his disciples saw "the destruction of all the dreams for the sake of which they had followed Jesus."[11] Only then did his followers recast the suffering, death, and failure of Jesus as a victory.

For all the differences in their conclusions about the man himself, Jefferson and Reimarus would have been in agreement about the character of those responsible for transforming the life and ministry of the Jesus of history into something else. As the founder of the Jesus Seminar Robert Funk summed up Reimarus's opinion, Reimarus "accuses the gospel writers of conscious fraud, fanaticism, and numerous contradictions."[12] So, too, these two sifters of the

Gospels both wrote eloquently and with evident exaspera-
tion that a few first-century scribes had foisted false history
onto succeeding generations, obscuring the living Jesus for
the sake of making him immortal. When Reimarus considered the injustice of this, Schweitzer noted, his language
"rises to heights of passionate feeling, and then it is as
though the fires of a volcano were painting lurid pictures
upon dark clouds. Seldom has there been a hate so eloquent,
so lofty a scorn."[13] And like the Jefferson Bible, as Funk
pointed out, Reimarus's "work was so controversial for his
day that he decided not to publish it himself."[14]

Reimarus's work was not the only attempt to reassess the
biography of Jesus made in Jefferson's lifetime. In his 1787
letter to his nephew Peter Carr, Jefferson urged that the former should "read all the histories of Christ," which, through
the years of the incubation of the Jefferson Bible, became a
crowded field. Schweitzer identified five works in particular which were marked by a "half developed rationalism":
History of the Last Three Years of the Life of Jesus by Johann
Jakob Hess (1768); Franz Volkmax Beinhard's *Essay upon
the Plan which the Founder of the Christian Religion adopted for the Benefit of Mankind* (1781); Johann Gottfried
Herder's *The Redeemer of men, as portrayed in our first three
Gospels* (1796); Ernst August Opitz's *History of Jesus, with a
Delineation of His Character* (1812); and Johann Adolph
Jakobi's *The History of Jesus for thoughtful and sympathetic
readers* (1816). These earliest efforts to recast the life of
Jesus in rational terms have little in common with *The Life
and Morals of Jesus of Nazareth*. For one, as Schweitzer
noted, "the sentimentality of [their] portraiture is bound-
less."[15] Unlike Jefferson, who was willing to admit that the

central figure of the Gospels was a man of his times and thus was limited in the ways any such man would be, in the writing of eighteenth- and early-nineteenth-century biographers, Jesus was perfect in every way. For Enlightenment-influenced authors, this meant that Jesus should be portrayed not as a man of his own time, but of theirs. For them, Schweitzer wrote:

> he must speak in a rational and modern fashion, and accordingly all His utterances are reproduced in a style of the most polite modernity. None of the speeches are allowed to stand as they were spoken; they are taken to pieces, paraphrased, and expanded, and sometimes, with the view of making them really lively, they are recast in the mould of a freely invented dialogue. In all these Lives of Jesus, not a single one of His sayings retains its authentic form.[16]

Closer to Jefferson's intentions, but published a decade and a half after he completed work on his *Life and Morals*, David Strauss for the first time sought to set aside the miraculous aspects of the New Testament in order to view its central figure in a new light in his *Life of Jesus*. Strauss was a pioneer of the school of German biblical studies which sought to examine the text in terms of its coherence; he did not take for granted, as theologians of previous generations did, that the multiple Gospel accounts of Jesus's ministry must ultimately be in agreement, despite their obvious contradictions. Instead, Strauss suggested that in every account there were different levels of truth: some might be regarded as close to a historical record, while others served a different purpose.

Unlike Jefferson and Reimarus, however, Strauss did not regard the Gospel writers as charlatans or hucksters, but rather as mouthpieces of early Christian communities seeking to reconcile myth and memory, applying supernatural interpretations to natural events. And while those earlier writers complained with great passion about the travesty that had occurred in the transformation of the words of Jesus into intentions he had never entertained, Strauss was content to dispassionately judge the process of each generation contending anew with scripture according to their own knowledge and sensibilities. For Strauss, that they so struggled was not a world-historical conspiracy to grant the imprimatur of tradition to outrageous untruths; it was simply the way these things work.

> Wherever a religion, resting upon written records, prolongs and extends the sphere of its dominion, accompanying its votaries through the varied and progressive stages of mental cultivation, a discrepancy between the representations of those ancient records, referred to as sacred, and the notions of more advanced periods of mental development, will inevitably sooner or later arise. In the first instance this disagreement is felt in reference only to the unessential—the external form: the expressions and delineations are seen to be inappropriate; but by degrees it manifests itself also in regard to that which is essential: the fundamental ideas and opinions in these early writings fail to be commensurate with a more advanced civilisation.[17]

Young Jefferson would have been glad to read Strauss, who diagnosed the crisis the former felt during the years he was imbibing Bolingbroke's pique, but presented a prescription that did not call for rejection of any passages of scripture, only a recalibration of expectations.

Each of these early reconsiderations of the life of Jesus—several before the Jefferson Bible and one after—serves here to suggest that Jefferson's project was part of a spectrum of approaches to the same question: What could be known of the Jesus of fact when only the Jesus of faith had been passed from one generation to the next? The early reconsiderations also serve as a reminder that many different versions of *The Life and Morals of Jesus of Nazareth* might have been fashioned out of the same materials. Only a close reading of the text Jefferson created can provide a full view of who he thought Jesus was.

* * *

The first words of *The Life and Morals of Jesus of Nazareth* are "Chapter Two." They appear at the top of the book's Greek, Latin, and English text columns, but are curiously left off the French. In each of these languages—Κεφ β, *Caput II, Chap II*—the heading is a reminder that Jefferson had no use for the for first chapter of any of the Gospels. Not for him were the cast-of-thousands genealogy of Matthew, the prophet Isaiah's evocation of a "voice crying out in the wilderness" found in Mark, the epistolary prologue or the angelic backstory of Luke, or perhaps least of all the cosmic poetry of *logos* and light offered by John.[18]

Jefferson's readers learn little of Jesus's infancy and nothing of his theodicy. It is as if Jesus was scarcely of interest before he reached the age of reason, and the notion that a man might have been present "in the beginning," as "the word" or in any other form, was contrary to the laws of nature. As Jefferson listed the Christian tropes he knew he must avoid:

the immaculate conception of Jesus, his deification, the creation of the world by him, his miraculous powers, his resurrection and visible ascension, his corporeal presence in the Eucharist, the Trinity; original sin, atonement, regeneration, election, orders of hierarchy, etc.[19]

That he apparently did not understand that the "immaculate conception" refers not to Jesus but to the sinless creation of Jesus's mother Mary in her own mother's womb does not speak well of Jefferson's general religious literacy. Nonetheless his point was clear: anything that could not have happened 1820 years after the birth of Christ Jefferson could not countenance as happening at the moment the *Anno Domini* clock began ticking. And so any suggestion that there should be some mystical origin of a poor first-century preacher much of the world had come to call God simply did not make the grade.

In place of any of this, Jefferson began his composite life of Jesus as prosaically as any politician might: with taxes. As the English text's section head, the one-line description of the events to come, put it: "The Roman empire taxed."

AND it came to pass in those days, that there went out a decree from Caesar Augustus, that all the world should be taxed. (And this taxing was first made when Cyrenius was governor of Syria.) And all went to be taxed, every one into his own city. And Joseph also went up from Galilee, out of the city of Nazareth, into Judaea, unto the city of David, which is called Bethlehem, (because he was of the house and lineage of David,) To be taxed with Mary his espoused wife, being great with child. And so it was, that, while they were there, the days were accomplished that she should be delivered. And she brought forth her firstborn son, and wrapped him in swaddling clothes, and laid him in a manger; because there was no room for them in the inn.[20]

With such a beginning, we see Jesus positioned within history and within a family, but decidedly not within theology. Starting thus might be seen simply as part of Jefferson's biographical imperative. As the title Jefferson would give to his book asserts, it was after all a "life of Jesus" before all else. But we should not gloss too quickly over the implicit critique of his source material this opening excision suggests. In omitting their very first words, Jefferson suggested, each of the Gospels got the story of Jesus remarkably, perhaps catastrophically, wrong. Recalling the terms of the "free exercise of reason" he hoped to apply to the Gospels, we might infer that Jefferson found in the New Testament's various beginnings nothing but a "ground work of vulgar ignorance, of things impossible, of superstitions, fanaticisms, & fabrications."[21]

This implication continues even with so seemingly straightforward a matter as Jesus's name. Following his birth, which no divine heralds announce or shepherds or magi attend, he is named by his parents with little fanfare:

AND when eight days were accomplished for the circumcising of the child, his name was called JESUS. And when they had performed all things according to the law of the Lord, they returned into Galilee, to their own city Nazareth.[22]

Immediately after "Jesus" in the text from which Jefferson cut (Luke 2:21), follow words which explain why this name was chosen: "which was so named of the angel before he was conceived in the womb." In *The Life and Morals of Jesus of Nazareth*, no angel named the infant who would later be called messiah and Christ. No messenger from God told Mary he would be born. Other than the undeniable inconvenience for his parents of giving birth to a child in a stable far from home (on tax day, no less), really nothing much happened at all.

Nor were certain elements of his childhood relevant to the story Jefferson's edit would tell. While the text does note, with words from Luke 2:40, "And the child grew, and waxed strong in spirit, filled with wisdom," Jefferson cut the verse short, leaving behind "and the grace of God was upon him." Similarly, a few lines later, Jefferson included the beginning of Luke 2:52, "And Jesus increased in wisdom and stature," but did not see fit to extend the description to its end: "and in favor with God and man."

Jefferson's treatment of the naming and youth of Jesus is indicative of his project throughout: No matter how essential such details may have seemed to readers of the Gospels down through the centuries, they were allowed by the redactor's blade only if they passed the test of reason. The supernatural, the miraculous, anything suggestive that Jesus might believe the divine things said about him—all of it had to go, especially when the fantastical might be replaced with the everyday.

Yet the avoidance of the miraculous and other suggestions of the divinity of Christ had unintended consequences for the text itself. After all, the miraculous nature of the life and ministry of Jesus is not incidental to the vast majority of the Gospels' readers, but rather their entire point.

We can see this clearly when Jefferson included elements of the ministry of Jesus to give some sense of how he spoke to the religious authorities of his day. In Jeffersonian fashion, his Jesus calls into question the authority of priests, and follows his own rules when he regards the strictures of tradition unjust. This is the case in a story which usually is told as "Healing the Man With the Withered Hand," a miracle meant to be illustrative that "Jesus is the Lord of the Sabbath," as the New International Version heads the relevant passage in the Gospel of Matthew.

As it is told in Matthew 12:1, Jesus and his disciples were passing through a corn field on the Sabbath when they became hungry and began to pick and eat the crops around them, though performing such labor was forbidden on the holy day of rest. This infraction does not go unnoticed:

> But when the Pharisees saw it, they said unto him, Behold, thy disciples do that which is not lawful to do upon the Sabbath day. But he said unto them, Have ye not read what David did, when he was an hungred, and they that were with him; How he entered into the house of God, and did eat the shew-bread, which was not lawful for him to eat, neither for them which were with him, but only for the priests? Or have ye not read in the law, how that on the Sabbath days the priests in the temple profane the Sabbath, and are blameless?

For Jefferson, this story proceeds along the lines of Matthew's account until the point when both Jesus and the Pharisees spot a man with a withered hand. The Pharisees ask if it is lawful to heal on the Sabbath, hoping to catch Jesus in a greater sin than picking corn. Jefferson's Jesus answers:

What man shall there be among you, that shall have one sheep, and if it fall into a pit on the Sabbath day, will he not lay hold on it, and lift it out? How much then is a man better than a sheep? Wherefore it is lawful to do well on the Sabbath days.

In the Gospel accounts, Jesus then commands the stricken man "Stretch out your hand," and when he does so, he is healed. Jefferson's Jesus does no such thing. Seeing the man, he asks the Pharisees if they would save their sheep, challenging them that if they would do so for an animal they should do more for a man. But Jesus himself does nothing. Moreover, while both the Gospel account and Jefferson's edit next say that the Pharisees soon "held a council against him" to determine "how they might destroy him," only in the full telling does this make narrative sense. No dramatic display of Jesus's spiritual gifts that might have elicited so strong a response is found in Jefferson's text. Nor does Jesus seem in this case a sufficiently forceful critic of religious authority to present much of a problem to the Pharisees, or anyone else. His insistence that it is lawful to heal on the Sabbath has far less disruptive power if Jesus does not then perform a healing on the Sabbath when given the opportunity.

Here and elsewhere any suggestion that Jesus may have performed miracles has been carefully excised, no matter the impression this creates of the man. Jefferson's Jesus seems to be able to heal but mostly chooses not to do so. Time and again, Jesus indicates that he might be able to perform a miracle of some kind, and then does nothing. While this no doubt made him more acceptable in Enlightenment circles, one imagines it would have made Jesus far less popular in Galilee.

In a passage taken from the ninth chapter of the Gospel of John, Jefferson's text presents Jesus and his disciples walking by a man blind from birth. His disciples ask, "Master, who did sin, this man, or his parents, that he was born blind?" To which Jesus replies, "Neither hath this man sinned, nor his parents: but that the works of God should be made manifest in him." In the Gospel account, Jesus then makes the works of God manifest by granting the man sight. In the Gospel according to Jefferson, however, the works of God are apparently simply that the man is blind and nothing can be done.

He may have imagined his *Life and Morals* as scripture shorn of all its unreasonable elements, but Jefferson's is a hard gospel. The blind do not see; the lame do not walk; the multitudes will remain hungry if loaves and fishes must be multiplied to feed them. Even those who look to Jesus for the forgiveness of sins are left wanting. This should not be surprising; Jefferson made clear in his letter to William Short that one of the differences between Jesus and himself was that Jesus "preaches the efficacy of repentance towards forgiveness of sin, I require a counterpoise of good works to redeem it."[23] Nonetheless, the decision to edit forgiveness from the life of Jesus can make him come across as not particularly Christlike.

In a section Jefferson included from the Gospel of Luke (7:36–46), Jesus is dining in the home of a Pharisee called Simon, when "a woman in the city" charges in to find him, carrying "an alabaster box of ointment."[24] Much to Simon's distress, the woman then washes Jesus's feet with her tears and dries them with her hair.

> Now when the Pharisee which had bidden him saw it, he spake within himself, saying, This man, if he were a prophet, would have known who and what manner of woman this is that touches him: for she is a sinner. And Jesus answering said unto him, Simon, I have somewhat to say unto thee. And he saith, Master, say on.[25]

Leaving aside the fact that Jefferson included the not-very-rational suggestion that Jesus could read Simon's mind, what follows is a further indication of the costs to the Gospel's appeal wrought by the litmus test of reason. In both Luke's and Jefferson's accounts, Jesus then tells his host a parable about debts owed and paid that makes it clear he regards the woman as more loved by him than his host, Simon. In only the unedited Gospel, however, Jesus then follows through with the climax of the story:

> "I tell you that her many sins are forgiven, so she showed great love. But the person who is forgiven only a little will love only a little."
>
> Then Jesus said to her, "Your sins are forgiven."
>
> The people sitting at the table began to say among themselves, "Who is this who even forgives sins?"
>
> Jesus said to the woman, "Because you believed, you are saved from your sins. Go in peace."

In forgiving her sins, Luke's Jesus answers the question "Who is this who even forgives sins?" by showing that he is one who claims the authority to do so. Jesus also suggests that belief alone is required for salvation. Jefferson's Jesus, meanwhile, speaks of forgiving sins, but does not actually do so, because Jefferson did not believe in that kind of forgiveness, as he expressed clearly to William Short.

This holds true throughout the text: Even in such settings where confession and absolution seem inseparable from certain scenes, Jefferson disregarded them. When John the Baptist is briefly introduced, Jefferson noted with Mark 1:4 "John did baptize in the wilderness." However, as with the naming and attributes of the young Jesus, the rest of the verse, and the point of John's ministry, did not make the cut: "and preach the baptism of repentance for the remission of sins." So, too, a few lines later, Jefferson's edit enlists one part of Matthew 3:5–6 to say of all those who came to see John:

> Then went out to him Jerusalem, and all Judaea, and all the region round about Jordan; And were baptized of him in Jordan.[26]

But again Jefferson left out the clause that explains why they all were there. "And were baptized of him in Jordan," Matthew 3:6 says, "confessing their sins."

In following closely Jefferson's account of Jesus's life, one begins to see that despite Jefferson's insistence that performing miracles and other divine attributes were later additions to an essential teaching, without them there is often not much to say about the immediate effect Jesus's ministry had on those around him. We are given chapter upon chapter of what Jefferson believed to be the words of Jesus, but no real sense of why anyone would have listened to him. With miracles hinted at but never delivered, forgiveness discussed but never offered, the text often has the feeling of a series of jokes without their punch lines. Jefferson's Jesus stories are all set up with no pay off.

Nowhere is this more true than in the case of the Gospels' biggest payoff of all: Christ's death and resurrection. Retelling the Passion according to the dictates of reason, Jefferson included only those verses that describe Jesus's suffering, none that suggest it is all occurring for a higher purpose. In the end, Jefferson's Jesus simply dies, and then his body is taken away. Drawn from Matthew 19 and 27, the last words of *The Life and Morals of Jesus of Nazareth* read:

> Now in the place where he was crucified there was a garden; and in the garden a new sepulchre, wherein never man yet laid.
>
> There laid they Jesus, and rolled a great stone to the door of the sepulchre, and departed.[27]

Throughout his explanations of why he felt someone should edit the New Testament, and continuing through his execution of that idea, Jefferson apparently never contended with the possibility that, without all the stories he rejected, it's unlikely we would have heard of Jesus at all. Counter to his intentions, Jefferson's contribution to the "life of Christ" genre may also be seen as a reinforcement of the notion that the teachings of Jesus of Nazareth, which Jefferson praised in the highest terms, are ultimately inseparable from the religious traditions upon which Jefferson heaped equal measures of disdain.

Yet any connection Jefferson's efforts might be said to have had to trends in late-nineteenth-century biblical criticism can only be seen in retrospect. As Jefferson did not want the book to be widely known, it had no immediate influence beyond his closest confidants, and so, in truth, initially it made no contribution at all.

With Jefferson's death six years after the completion of *The Life and Morals of Jesus of Nazareth*, the book ceased to be the useful compendium to which its maker alone often turned. However, the text would soon begin a new and markedly different phase of its existence—as an object of public fascination. Before that occurred, though, it was all but forgotten. In a sense, the Jefferson Bible was buried beneath the myth and memory of the man, much as he imagined the true teachings of Jesus to be.

Lost and Found

Great religious books are often inseparable from tales of their discovery. Whether it is Joseph Smith unearthing the golden plates that would become the Book of Mormon, or the Bedouin shepherds Muhammad edh-Dhib, Jum'a Muhammad, and Khalil Musa stumbling upon the cave-hidden jars that yielded the Dead Sea Scrolls, part of the significance of certain sacred texts is derived from narratives presenting the possibility that they might have never been known at all. Whether born in legend or in history, such narratives foreground a found text's importance by suggesting it was brought to light only by providence, or perhaps dumb luck.

The Life and Morals of Jesus of Nazareth is such a book. While it remained a subject of anecdote and rumor for much of the nineteenth century, and while certain members of the Jefferson family were aware that a compendium of scripture had served as their esteemed forbearer's nightly reading at Monticello, the world would likely not know more about it if not for the work of a single man, who happened to have the skills, interests, and connections necessary to appreciate and make something of what he had found.

Dr. Cyrus Adler was the son of an Arkansas shopkeeper and cotton farmer who, in a quintessentially American story of reinvention, ended up first as a professor of Semitic languages at Johns Hopkins University and later as one of the most influential public historians of his generation. He helped found the American Jewish Historical Society, and eventually became an advisor on religious issues to presidents. In this latter role Adler became perhaps the first person to pass up a visit to the White House because it happened to fall on the Sabbath. An observant Jew, he was summoned to meet with Theodore Roosevelt on a Saturday in 1904 to discuss the rising dangers faced by Jews around the world. Though this opportunity arose at the height of the Dreyfus Affair and in the shadow of the Kishinev pogrom, Adler declined to break the prohibition against working on *shabbat*. As the first president to appoint a Jew to a cabinet post, Roosevelt did not feel snubbed but rather understood the position in which his invitation had put Adler. The day of the meeting was changed, and that same year Adler published an edited volume of American responses to violence against Jews in Russia, which included an impassioned statement by Roosevelt himself.

Before reaching such heights of influence, Adler served as a curator, librarian, and Director of the Division of Religion at the Smithsonian Institution, which put him in the position to discover and collect examples of the material culture of American religion. It was this mandate that ultimately transformed *The Life and Morals of Jesus of Nazareth* into the Jefferson Bible.

While the Smithsonian today is made up of eighteen museums, when Adler joined the institution at the end of the nineteenth century it had just one: the United States National Museum, which occupied what is now the Arts and Industries Building on the National Mall in Washington, DC. Organized into four vast pavilions surrounding a grand rotunda, the U.S. National Museum was the Smithsonian's first site dedicated to displaying scientific and historical objects gathered through its mission to "increase and diffuse" knowledge.

Adler had initially visited the building upon completing his studies at Johns Hopkins University in Baltimore. Having made the journey to the capital to view an exhibition of photographs of cuneiform inscriptions, he was disappointed to discover that he had arrived after the exhibit had been taken down for reframing. Undeterred, Adler talked his way into a back room to view the photographs, and left the museum with a job.[1]

Appointed Honorary Assistant Curator of Semitics in 1888, Adler soon rose to Curator of Historic Archaeology and Historic Religions (1889–1908), then to Institute Librarian (1892–1905), and finally to Assistant Secretary of the Smithsonian (1905–1908). Concurrently serving as Director of the Division of Religion, established in 1890, Adler's purview included the collection of objects related not only to the religious past, but also to the religious present.

This wide focus was a quiet revolution in terms of how religion traditionally had been treated in museums. As Adler later wrote of the early days of the Division of Religion:

At that time the tendency in museums abroad, and to a certain extent among the students of the history of religions generally, was to deal only with the religious

CHAPTER 4

practices and ideas of the semi-civilized or barbarous nations, and to treat but sparingly those of the more civilized and cultivated nations of the earth. It was determined, in taking up the subject here, to adopt a course contrary to that hitherto followed, and to endeavor, from the educational point of view, to interest the people in the history of religion by leading them to the unknown, as it were, in the terms of the known.[2]

Adler began to pursue collections initially from the traditions he assumed late-nineteenth-century museum visitors would be most aware. As he described it:

Accordingly, the first three religions to which attention was given were Judaism, Christianity, and Mohammedanism, in the order of their respective establishments. Other religions were later illustrated, especially Brahmanism and Buddhism.

The hand-written collecting notes made by Adler and his colleagues around this time provide a fascinating view into what this early effort in documenting a wide spectrum of religious history looked like on the ground. One page, for example, includes a "drum for dervishes," a number of Jewish ceremonial garments, and a photo album from a pilgrimage to Mecca, all of which were collected in Boston.[3]

Adler's main space for displaying such items was in the National Museum's west hall, which he filled with display cases, eight feet high and twenty feet long. The religion section soon contained eight cases for Judaism, six for Christianity, six for Buddhism, three for Islam, three for Hinduism, one for Shintoism, and one for Zoroastrianism. Another three cases held a collection of amulets, a collection of rosaries, and a garment he labeled a "Korean sorcerer's outfit."

Adler's goal was to present a "difficult subject," as he referred to religion, through a rigorous historical and scientific method. "The religious ideas have been described through objects or examples of ceremony," he wrote in describing his approach. "The professors of each creed have received full faith and their own explanations of the ideas involved in a given ceremony have been adopted."[4]

This approach had its limitations. As one Smithsonian report lamented, "The amount of space supplied is unfortunately altogether inadequate for the collection, resulting in an overcrowded arrangement and preventing the installation of much important material which remains in storage."[5]

Yet Adler, as ever, was undeterred. When the West Hall was full, objects from the Division of Religion moved into other spaces within the museum, including the prized real estate of the rotunda, where large sculptural figures of Buddha and Vishnu stood alongside Armed Freedom, a copy of the statue atop the U.S. Capitol Building.

Before we jump to the conclusion that this represented an early public show of support for American religious diversity by the federal government, it is worth noting that when Congress created the Smithsonian in 1846 it was to collect "all objects of natural history, plants, & geological & mineralogical specimens" along with "all objects of art and of foreign and curious research."[6] It might be said that, initially, the nation's museum largely consider religion to be "foreign and curious." Early Smithsonian reports even stated that "obviously" only Catholicism and the Orthodox church would be included in the Christianity cases.[7] When crowds gathered at the National Museum to view religion behind glass, it was presumed that the demographically dominant gaze of American Protestantism was looking in.

The working assumption behind this was that religious expressions could be neatly divided into categories the publications of US National Museum referred to as "creed and cult," with the understanding that "it is the cult which most readily lends itself to museum exhibition."[8]

Even Cyrus Adler, or perhaps especially Cyrus Adler, the son of an Arkansas Jewish shop-keeping cotton farmer, understood that, in the American context at that time, there were religious ideas seen as normative, and those regarded as something else, and only the latter should be put behind glass. Perhaps for this reason, he won praise from certain quarters for his approach to exhibiting religious objects. An 1893 edition of the magazine *Biblical World* assessed the future of religion at the Smithsonian this way: "With the admirable facilities possessed by a government institution for obtaining objects from all parts of the world, the scope of this section ought at an early day to be made coequal with the universe."[9]

Adler was not content to collect objects "from all parts of the world," however. Just as he had insisted that religion must be presented in terms of both the unknown and the known, he also considered the distinctive religious cultures of the United States to be within the scope of his responsibilities. While Adler was busy tracking down objects showing a range of geographically distant beliefs and practices that must have seemed exotic to many when displayed in Washington in the 1890s, he was also trying to solve a mystery closer to home.

Several years before, while still completing his doctoral studies, Adler had been hired to catalogue a private library. As he later recounted it:

> In 1886 I was engaged, when a fellow at Johns Hopkins University, Baltimore, in cataloguing a small but very valuable Hebrew library gathered together by Dr. Joshua I. Cohen.[10]

The Baltimore Cohens were among Maryland's most storied Jewish families. With American roots beginning before the Revolution, they achieved considerable success in business in Richmond and Charleston. After having settled in Baltimore early in the nineteenth century, they were sufficiently established by the 1820s to make major political contributions, including pressing for passage of the so-called "Jew Bill" which sought "to extend to the sect of people professing the Jewish religion the same rights and privileges that are enjoyed by Christians."[11]

Joshua Cohen had been dead sixteen years by the time Adler first visited his library, but what the young scholar found there was the living embodiment of a broad and searching mind. "Doctor Cohen was a man of scholarly and scientific attainments, and throughout his life held relation with the scientific world, being perhaps best known as a mineralogist," Adler wrote. "His tastes, which were also literary, historical and antiquarian, led him to the formation of various collections illustrative of his studies."[12] Cohen's cabinets displayed samples of minerals, colonial and continental currency, an array of autographs, and a selection of Hebrew literature which, though considered "small" by Adler, was extensive enough to fill a published catalogue nearly fifty pages long. But no matter how eclectic Cohen's collections, there was no indication what the most consequential find by Adler would be.

> Amongst the books were two copies of the New Testament mutilated which contained on the inside of the cover a newspaper slip giving an account of what Jefferson had undertaken.

That clipping, glued in place inside the front cover, was from a widely reprinted report, which throughout August 1853 appeared in newspapers in states including Ohio, North Carolina, Alabama, Pennsylvania, Indiana, and Vermont, as well as Lancashire, England.

> Mr. Jefferson made an original book out of the New Testament, an account of which is given by him in a letter to John Adams, dated October 13, 1813, when Jefferson was seventy years old. He took two Copies of the New Testament and cut out the sayings of the Saviour, rejecting every verse which was not evidently his; these he pasted in a book, and his compilation is described as covering forty-six pages. He wrote old John Adams, that this arrangement has placed before him "the most sublime and benevolent code of morals ever offered to man."[13]

Nearly everywhere it appeared, the clipping began with the words "A Curious Book," but interestingly not in the account pasted into the damaged New Testament Adler had discovered. Beneath the clipping, in Joshua Cohen's tidy hand, there followed an explanation of how the books came to be in Baltimore:

This and the corresponding vol. are the identical copies alluded to in the above article. They were purchased by me at the sale of Dr. Macaulay's Medical Library, by whom they had been bought at the sale of Mr. Jefferson's library.

See letter to John Adams,
Jefferson 's Works, Vol. vi, 217.
JOSHUA I. COHEN.

Cohen's note did not provide all the answers to questions Adler may have had. To begin with, it remains unknown what Cohen might have meant by "Dr. Macaulay's Medical Library." As the University of Virginia Library Bulletin stated in 1916, as far as Jefferson scholars know, "there was no sale at which these Testaments could have purchased by Dr. Macaulay."[14] Yet Adler rightly recognized these "mutilated" copies of the New Testament as pieces to a puzzle.

"That Jefferson had in mind the preparation of such a book, and that he actually prepared it, has been known to students of his letters and writings," Adler wrote. Yet in the decades since Jefferson's death, scant evidence of the book had survived. When mentioned at all, the book had appeared as an anecdote of his supposed piety, in the words of those eager to refute aspersions cast upon his memory.

The first such public instance of its invocation had occurred in the 1840s, when the spirit of religious revival known as the Second Great Awakening had led some to question why there was no chapel on the grounds of the University of Virginia, founded by Jefferson during the last years of his life. As recounted in the *Richmond Enquirer* in 1847:

The press have teemed with attacks upon the memory of Mr. Jefferson, for his imputed designs of depriving the University of Virginia of the benefit of all moral and religions influences. A friend of Mr. Jefferson, and of the noble institution which he has left as his last, best legacy of his native state, has most properly felt himself called upon, in justice to Mr. J. and to the University, to refute a late attack of the character alluded to.[15]

This unnamed friend had urged that anyone attacking Jefferson:

> might have been shown the chamber of Jefferson in a suite of rooms [at Monticello] on the first floor opening on the southern brow of the mountain, delightful for their cheerful light and ventilation. He might have had pointed out to him the spot where, ever at hand, stood his beautifully bound copy of the "Morals of Jesus," textually extracted by himself, exhibiting to the glance of the eye each verse in four languages. He might have been told that it was his habit nightly to seek in its perusal composure of mind from worldly cares.[16]

Ten years later, Jefferson's biographer Henry S. Randall also noted that toward the end of Jefferson's life, "the book oftenest chosen for reading for an hour or half an hour before going to bed was a collection of extracts from the Bible." Randall went on to describe it: "In a handsome moroccobound volume, labeled on the back, 'Morals of Jesus,' lie placed the parallel texts in four languages."[17]

Yet despite these occasional references to *The Life and Morals of Jesus of Nazareth*, no one before Adler seems to have come across the raw material of its creation. The two highly edited English New Testaments he discovered were thus as enticing to him as a map to a long-buried treasure. Adler made initial inquiries into the location of the book these other damaged scriptures had made, but to no avail.

The discovery seems to have gnawed at Adler, however. Four years later, now employed by the Smithsonian, Adler was well positioned to take note of a report issued by Congress, which was then considering another acquisition related to Jefferson's literary endeavors. This proposed sale, along with others preceding it, may provide a further explanation as to why *The Life and Morals* remained so long out of view.

Since the purchase of the Monticello library by Congress in 1815, Jefferson's heirs had made multiple attempts to sell collections of his correspondence, manuscripts, and other papers. In 1848, Jefferson's eldest grandson, Thomas Jefferson Randolph, offered to make all public and private papers available to the federal government, but was rebuffed by then-Secretary of State James Buchanan. Agreeing to vet the collection, but insisting that only Jefferson's public papers would be considered for purchase, Buchanan directed Randolph to send the entire collection to the State Department, which would sort those papers of interest from those that would be returned. Through the decade that followed, Jefferson's papers were moved from Washington to Williamsburg and back again. Many were lost, unbound, or declared "refuse matter." In 1869, Randolph notified the State Department that he still had not received the personal papers not included in the purchase. Two years later, three boxes containing thousands of items were returned to the family.[18]

It was many of these papers, and perhaps others not originally offered for sale, that Randolph's daughter Sarah Randolph offered to Congress in 1890. Though the sale never came to be, the proposal included a listing of the materials to be acquired, which ended up having lasting significance on Jefferson's legacy.

Reading the report, Adler noted the words of Librarian of Congress Ainsworth R. Spofford, who described a work he called " *'The Morals and Life of Jesus of Nazareth,' extracted textually from the Gospels in Greek, Latin, French and English.*" The description continued:

> Title and very full index in his own hand. Texts were cut by him out of printed copies of Greek, Latin, French and English Testaments and pasted in this book of blank pages, which was handsomely bound in red morocco, ornamented in gilt, and titled on the back in gilt letters, 'The Morals of Jesus.' His original idea was to have the life and teachings of the Saviour, told in similar excerpts, prepared for the Indians, thinking this simple form would suit them best. But, abandoning this, the formal execution of his plan took the shape above described, which was for his individual use. He used the four languages that he might have the texts in them side by side, convenient for comparison. In the book he pasted a map of the ancient world and the Holy Land, with which he studied the New Testament.[19]

Armed with this new information, Adler renewed his search. He went now directly to the Jefferson family and learned that upon Sarah Randolph's death in 1892, *The Life and Morals of Jesus of Nazareth* had come into the possession of her daughter, Carolina Ramsey Randolph, Jefferson's great-granddaughter. On behalf of the Smithsonian, Adler made her an offer of $400, which she accepted.

By then it had been nearly a decade since he first discovered the mutilated New Testaments in the Cohen library. If Adler had not acted swiftly when he finally located the book, it may have never come to light, much less as quickly as it did. Within three years, Carolina Randolph would sell off more than seven thousand items from the Jefferson collection. Other papers passed to her nieces upon her death in 1902; some of those were later destroyed in a fire. There is no telling where a peculiar scrapbook of Gospel verses might have ended up had Adler not acted when he did, but certainly not in the hands of the U.S. National Museum.

And it was as a museum object first of all that Adler hoped to acquire the book. He wanted it not just because it was a prized artifact of the third president, but because at that time he was curating a very broad and somewhat unusual exhibit on the Bible. Even as his exhibits in the US National Museum were affirming the idea that the "cult" dimension of religion was appropriate for display while the "creed" dimension was not, Adler was planning another exhibit that put the creedal foundations of American religion behind glass.

* * *

In an exhibit staged at the Cotton States International Exposition, held in Atlanta in 1895, Adler presented a huge range of objects to introduce American audiences to the places, ideas, cultures, and texts necessary to consider the history, development, and contemporary relevance of the Bible. It was, Adler said, "the first collection put together at an exposition which attempted to show in outline all of the possibilities of study in this most important field."[20]

In a single, large room, Adler managed to fit an exhibit containing examples of geological specimens of Bible lands, such as "Dust from Jerusalem" and "Water from the Jordan"; biblical flora including "Seed pods of the Carob tree," "Sycamore from Palestine," "Apples of Sodom," "Unripe pomegranate from Palestine," and "Cone of the cedar of Lebanon"; and biblical fauna including bats, monkeys, camels, gazelles, mice, a dozen species of birds, three species of lizards, and six species of insects. Adler also featured musical instruments including a round tabret, a four-side tabret, a kettledrum, a ram's horn, and cymbals, as well as various costumes, and a handful of mummies, both animal and human. There were also of course a great many Bibles, broadly defined: texts ranging from Hebrew fragments to medieval manuscripts to that most American of scriptures, Jefferson's razor blade translation.

The newly acquired *The Life and Morals of Jesus of Nazareth* appeared in a section of modern translations of the Bible, of which it was the most modern of all:

The New Testament, translated by John Wycliffe
Tyndale's New Testament
The Gothic and Anglo-Saxon Gospels
Coverdale's Bible
The Genevan Version
King James or Authorized Version
The Revised Version
Parallel New Testament

The New Testament, translated by Tischendorf
Luther's Bible
Spanish Old Testament
Eliot's Indian Bible
Miniature Bible
Cromwell's Soldier's Pocket Bible
Hieroglyphic Bible
Bishop Asbury's Testament
Thomas Jefferson's Bible

In the exhibition's catalogue, Adler's description of the book further made the case that it was appropriately included among translations.

Thomas Jefferson's Bible, consisting of texts from the Evangelists, historically arranged.—This book bears the title, "The life and morals of Jesus of Nazareth, extracted textually from the gospels, in Greek, Latin, French, and English." Four versions were employed. The passages were cut out of printed copies and pasted in the book. A concordance of the texts is given in the front and the sources of the verses in the margins. The section of the Roman law under which Jefferson supposed Christ to have been tried is also cited. All of these annotations, as well as the title page and concordance, are in Jefferson's own handwriting. Two maps, one of Palestine and another of the ancient world, are pasted in the front. Jefferson long had the preparation of this book in mind. On January 29, 1804, he wrote from Washington to Dr. Priestley: "I had sent to Philadelphia to get two Testaments (Greek) of the same edition, and two English, with a design to cut out the morsels of morality and paste them on the leaves of book." Nearly ten years later (October 13, 1813), in writing to John Adams, he stated that he had for his own use cut up the gospels "verse by verse" out of the printed book, arranging the matter which is evidently His (Christ's). In the same letter he describes the book as "the most sublime and benevolent code of morals which has ever been offered to man."[21]

Adler's descriptive text for use in the exhibition provides the first instance in which *The Life and Morals* became subtly transformed into "Thomas Jefferson's Bible." Identifying the book this way, Adler performed something of a sleight of hand. It was not, after all, a full Bible. Nor was it the lone example of scripture that Jefferson had owned, as the suggestion that it was "Thomas Jefferson's Bible" implied.

Thanks to this framing, though *The Life and Morals of Jesus of Nazareth* was just one item among thousands displayed, the Exposition proved to be the Jefferson Bible's coming out party. Typical of the coverage its display received, an article in the *Atlanta Constitution* foregrounded the grandeur of the exhibition overall, and then narrowed its focus to the surprising star of the show. As its headline read:

HUGE DISPLAY THIS

Extensive Exhibit of the Smithsonian
Institute at the Exposition

TO ECLIPSE ALL FORMER EXHIBITS[22]

The article went on to note that, along with such fascinating displays as "The First Steamship to Cross the Atlantic"

and "the First One Hundred Miles of Railway Built in Georgia," visitors would be delighted to discover there were plentiful Bibles to be found among marvels of the modern world.
Moreover, the article noted:

> In the next alcove will be found an exhibition which, for
> want of a better name, may be called a collection illustra-
> tive of biblical archaeology. This collection was arranged
> by Dr. Cyrus Adler with especial reference to the well-
> known interest of the Georgia people in matters of Bible
> history.[23]

After dutifully noting the dozens of antiquities to be
seen, the report focused on an item that had evidently become among the most popular attractions.

> The gem of the collection, to many minds, will be
> Thomas Jefferson's Bible, a composite book prepared by
> the great Virginian by clipping from four versions of the
> New Testament—Greek, Latin, French, and English—
> and arranging the clippings so as to make it a consecutive
> history of Jesus Christ, and also a systematic presentation
> of the Christian philosophy as developed in the canoni-
> cal books.

Such was the spectacle of the Exposition that newspapers far from Atlanta published descriptions of their own,
with many similarly granting the most attention to the book
whose given title was even then receding into the back-
ground. "Bible students will be interested in the announce-
ment that a collection of valuable articles Illustrative of Biblical archaeology will be one of the features of the Cotton
States Exposition at Atlanta," reported the *Democrat and*

Chronicle of Rochester, New York. "The collection has been prepared by Dr. Cyrus Adler and is placed on exhibition by the Smithsonian Institution. Nothing like it has ever been attempted before."[24] In New York, too, "Thomas Jefferson's Bible" was regarded as the highlight of the exhibit. Though fourteen lines of type are devoted to the book's description, its true name nowhere appears in the report. With similar accounts published as far away as Louisiana and Missouri, the book's journey to national renown was well underway.

To be sure, an Orthodox Jew so observant of the religious laws of Judaism that he declined a meeting with a president was an unlikely champion of a scrapbook of New Testament verses. Yet seen more broadly within Adler's long career not only as the steward of a national collection of religious objects, but also as an advocate for religious equality and freedom, it makes sense. Adler's curation of the Bible exhibition at the Cotton States Exposition drew on his deep experience as a scholar of biblical languages, but moreover it provided him with an opportunity to subtly subvert some of the very guidelines he had established for displaying religion at the U.S. National Museum.

Intentionally or not, the exhibition strategy of distinguishing between "creed" and "cult" at the museum in Washington had helped reinforce an understanding that the paradigmatic creedal perspective—that is, the Protestant perspective—was the default religious view. Those guided by "creed" were allowed to stand on the outside of religion display cases to assess the "cult" practices shown within. Yet given an opportunity to present an exhibition beyond the museum's walls, Adler decided to put the foundation of that perspective under a microscope, asking Bible-believing

Americans to subject their assumptions to the same kind of scrutiny. The book he had come to call "Thomas Jefferson's Bible" was after all an object with questions of "creed" at its core. With every cut and paste, Jefferson had asked himself what he believed. Moreover, to see this uniquely American scripture displayed along with biblical antiquities was to present the entwined possibilities that religious objects created in the United States were part of a long lineage, even as they represented something new and unexpected.

Thirty-seven years after the Cotton States Exposition, in 1932, Adler was asked to present remarks on the "American religious scene" at the National Conference of Catholics, Jews, and Protestants, held in Washington. As the theme of the seminar at which he spoke was Religious Liberty and Mutual Understanding, he might have provided his perspective as a member of a religious minority in a majority Christian nation. Instead, Adler did something far bolder by declaring that such categories should not matter at all in America.

> The beginning of the Republic meant the end of any kind of established Church in America and hence the end of any domination or of even an especially favored position by a religious majority. So far as matters of religion are concerned there are no majorities or minorities. All people may worship God according to the dictates of their own conscience with reference to the question as to whether the particular form of worship or belief has many followers or few. This is the most important thought I have to bring to the present discussion. It is fundamental. Unless it be accepted all of our discussions

92   CHAPTER 4

will be in vain, and I hope that I have made the idea sufficiently clear without the necessity of spending further words upon it.[25]

Those were not quite Adler's final words on the subject, however. As if underscoring that this notion was not his alone, Adler went on to quote one of the most significant early statements of American religious liberty, offered by George Washington to the Hebrew Congregation of Newport, Rhode Island, in 1790:

The Citizens of the United States of America have a right to applaud themselves for having given to mankind examples of an enlarged and liberal policy: a policy worthy of imitation. All possess alike liberty of conscience and immunities of citizenship. It is now no more that toleration is spoken of, as if it was by the indulgence of one class of people, that another enjoyed the exercise of their inherent natural rights. For happily the Government of the United States, which gives to bigotry no sanction, to persecution no assistance, requires only that they who live under its protection should demean themselves as good citizens, in giving it on all occasions their effectual support.

No matter if you are a member of a vast church, or a tiny temple, or a sect unto yourself, as Jefferson claimed to be, Adler insisted, religious liberty should have nothing to do with numbers, and less to do with toleration, as if permission must be granted to believe what you believe.

For Adler, the spirit of this creed was captured in *The Life and Morals of Jesus of Nazareth*. As a museum curator, he saw it primarily as an object to be displayed. By adding it to the national collection, and by showing it in the company of other objects similar or different, to varying degrees, Jefferson's scrapbook at once presented the internal diversity of American religion and underscored the notion that in the United States even the act of mutilating scripture might be not just tolerated, but embraced.

Born Again

As the story began to be told in the first spring of the new century, Representative John Fletcher Lacey was giving the collection of Jefferson's books purchased by Congress in 1815 a "careful examination" when he thought to inquire about the whereabouts of the Jefferson Bible.[1]

A devout Christian and an admirer of the third president, Lacey's request would not have seemed unusual. He was in general thought to be a man who liked to get to the bottom of things. When he was a sergeant major in the Union Army a quarter century before, Lacey had endeavored to learn and remember the name of every man in Iowa's Thirty-third regiment, and he was still regarded as "naturally a gentleman of an investigative turn of mind."[2]

Though it was said that Lacey nearly ransacked the Library of Congress in the search that followed, the book was, to his surprise, nowhere among the volumes that had been brought so carefully from Monticello eighty-five years before. Only upon asking for the assistance of the Librarian of Congress, Ainsworth Spofford, did Lacey learn that the volume would be found not in the shelves serving the

Capitol, but a little further up the National Mall, in the library of the Smithsonian.

"A few days later," a 1904 account recalled, "Mr. Lacey sought the librarian of the national museum and queried him concerning this mysterious volume, the gift of Thomas Jefferson."[3]

That it was not precisely a gift is just one of many details that might have given pause to any who knew the circumstances of the book's acquisition by the federal government, but such quibbling would only get in the way of a good story. The account continued:

> The aged librarian listened to Major Lacey's inquiry and then said he might be able to throw some light on the subject. Going down into a wallet he drew from an exclusive apartment a bit of a key. With this the librarian proceeded to a private case not open to public inspection, and fitting the key, opened the cabinet and drew from a recess a volume.

Far from the display cases of the museum's crowded religion section or its airy rotunda, presumably in a dusty back room that few but Congressman Lacey had the fortitude to reach, according to the story the elderly librarian then held out a book with red leather covers.

"I fancy this is what you are looking for," he allegedly said.

Lacey studied the volume and ran his fingers over the gilt "Morals of Jesus" embossed on its spine. Yes, he replied, it was indeed. He opened the book's delicate pages and studied the four columns of text before handing it back to the librarian, assuring him he would soon return.

As the story usually concludes, shortly after leaving the Smithsonian that day, Lacey brought the book to the attention of the House Committee on Printing. He urged his colleagues to consider having this long-forgotten collection of Gospel extracts reproduced. With only a little persuasion, the next stage of the life of the Jefferson Bible had begun.

Though this account captures the rough chronology of the journey of *The Life and Morals of Jesus of Nazareth* toward its initial publication, it is also a further indication of the ways tales of discovery tend to embroider the truth.

Lacey himself was the first person to tell one version of this story, in a short essay detailing his search that was published in newspapers across the country beginning in May of 1900. It did not matter that just five years earlier the book's display at the Cotton States Exposition had been covered extensively; many of the headlines above this new report declared triumphantly "Jefferson's Bible Found."[4]

In addition to printing Lacey's words, many newspapers reported with greater or lesser levels of detail on the congressman's deeds—the supposedly single-minded quest that had led to his great discovery. As it was written in Des Moines:

Just how long the Jefferson Bible might have remained in obscurity but for the efforts of Major Lacey cannot be estimated, but it is not difficult to believe that but for the Iowa congressman this remarkable volume might never have been rescued from oblivion.[5]

And it was not only Iowans who gave him the credit. The *San Francisco Chronicle* noted:

Clergy and laity will be interested in knowing that through the diligent search of Representative Lacey of Iowa what is known as the Jefferson Bible has been brought to light. This interesting book is now in an iron safe at the National Museum.[6]

The "iron safe" was a considerable upgrade to the wooden cabinet elsewhere described, just one embellishment among many that became attached to the book's second discovery within a decade.

It is worth noting a few of the more dubious claims that contributed to the Jefferson Bible mythology in those early days of its public career. Had Lacey truly gone looking for the book among the original library Jefferson sold to Congress, he might have discovered that in fact very few of those 6,487 books remained. Two-thirds had been lost in a fire in 1851. Moreover, the contents of that collection were all well known, and *The Life and Morals* had never been listed among them. This was not due to some conspiracy to keep it hidden, but, of course, because *The Life and Morals* had not yet been created at the time of the sale. And if Lacey did indeed ask the Librarian of Congress for help, Spofford might have told him that Congress had considered acquiring the book on his recommendation ten years before but had declined, or that it was no great mystery where the book could be found for it had recently been on display in both Atlanta and Washington. Finally, as Lacey was approaching sixty years old in 1900, he surely would have noticed that the "aged librarian" Cyrus Adler was then all of 36.

Some of the growing legend surrounding the book's supposed discovery was likely Lacey's doing, but it had more to do with general public excitement that this heretofore mostly unknown relic of the founding fathers was now coming to light, and the eagerness of the press to make a tale of mystery and detection out of a congressman's uneventful trip to the National Museum.

Though Lacey's role in the finding of a book that was no longer lost was certainly overstated, the part he played in its publication was indeed significant. Cyrus Adler had seen the book from a museum curator's perspective—as a curious and singular artifact of a remarkable American life. For his purposes of crafting exhibits, the red leather-bound object was sufficient. It was, to paraphrase the poet Wallace Stevens, the thing itself, rather than ideas about the thing, which any reproduction was bound to become. For Adler, publishing the volume was, at first, of little importance. Lacey, on the other hand, saw it first of all as a Christian and secondly as an admirer of Jefferson. As each, Lacey had an evangelical zeal.

Born in West Virginia but raised in Iowa, Lacey had grappled with religious matters all his life. When his Quaker mother sought to marry his father, a Methodist, it caused a religious rift in the family that echoed down through generations. She adopted Methodism and reared her son in the faith. Thanks in part to her influence, from early days he had sought to understand the larger history of his church and its heroes, as he recounted in his autobiography.

> The first book of any size that I ever read was Daubigne's *History of the Reformation,* which I read aloud to mother while she sewed and patched and darned and did the household work for a young and growing family. The "Diet at Worms" struck me as very amusing, but I became

a partisan of Luther in my childhood, and have always admired his sturdy independence ever since.[7]

Next Lacey had turned to John Foxe's *Actes and Monuments*, also known as the *Book of Martyrs*. He counted it as a "logical sequel" to the *History of the Reformation*; it was, Lacey somewhat sardonically recalled, a "cheerful volume" to read at his mother's knee. From there he borrowed every book available in town, carefully covering each with paper and using thumb papers to keep his excited hands from smudging any of the type.

Perhaps Lacey's most surprising and formative religious memory was a chance trip to Cincinnati's Western Museum, which through the middle decades of the nineteenth century featured a massive display depicting a Dantean vision of hell, presented with dozens of human-scale wax figures. "Infernal Regions" created by the sculptor Hiram Powers, who would later achieve international fame for his marble sculpture *The Greek Slave*, offered visitors to the Western Museum the opportunity to walk through a netherworld set in an upper story exhibit hall crammed full with all manner of frightening sights. As Lacey remembered:

> There was a clashing of chains, a roaring of furnaces, diabolical noises, and a variety of demons and condemned souls that I can yet see in my memory. While standing at an iron railing looking at the horrible vision, a charge of electricity went through the railing throwing us all on our knees.[8]

This last was not hyperbole. When Powers had noticed his wax figures were suffering from the hands of too many too-curious exhibit-goers, he had affixed several signs about the museum, "written in flame-colored letters and couched in the choicest bugaboo phraseology," as another witness put it, "warning all such indiscreet persons that the denizens of the Infernal Regions could not be touched by mortal hands with impunity, and that immediate punishment would visit transgressors."[9]

When this failed to protect the soft wax figures from pressing hands of visitors who naturally were only more fervently enticed by this warning, Powers ran the statues through with electric wires, which delivered a shock strong enough to knock patrons to their knees. Along with protecting the display, this had another practical effect, as Lacey recalled. "A constant stream of visitors was passing through the building," he wrote, "and the electric shock seemed to be sufficient to clear the way for more visitors."

From these few glimpses at his childhood, we might surmise that Lacey had an affinity for books, for the religious-independence of Luther, for those willing to risk all for a spiritual cause, and perhaps for the peculiar turns American religion might take.

If Lacey saw all this in the Jefferson Bible when he first encountered it in 1900 it may also have been because he held the third president in the highest esteem. Assessing the many criticisms endured by Jefferson, particularly those offered by his contemporaries who regarded as an unconstitutional overreach the Louisiana Purchase, Lacey noted that "Providence raises statesmen from time to time who see beyond the narrow horizon of their own time."[10]

Though he credited Jefferson with this sort of vision, Lacey did not go so far as to agree with him on religious matters. Yet that even one who doubted the divinity of Christ could find so much of use in the Gospels as to create his own scrapbook of Jesus's teachings was proof to Lacey that *The Life and Morals* might be useful to modern readers.

> Mr. Jefferson was a freethinker, but his clear and just mind appreciated the teachings of the founder of the Christian religion, and the study of the Scriptures was the frequent occupation of his busy mind. He read Marcus Aurelius, Epictetus, and other ancient writers on moral philosophy, and he conceived the idea of condensing the life and teachings of Jesus into a small volume, in which everything of a supernatural character should be omitted, evidently believing that the great truths of the religion of our Saviour would lose nothing by being separated from the miracles and wonders with which they are accompanied in the text of the Gospels.[11]

Lacey continued:

> It has been said by an eminent minister of the gospel that Christianity must be true or it could never have survived so much poor preaching. Mr. Jefferson has put it to a still better test by this abridgment of the doctrines of the Divine Author.

Two years after he had first encountered the book, Lacey put forward a bill calling for the U.S. government to fund the printing of 9,000 copies—3,000 for use in the Senate, 6,000 for use in the House—to be reproduced "by photolithographic process," and with an introduction "not to exceed 25 pages," which would be written by Dr. Cyrus Adler. The estimated expense for this project was $3,227.[12]

While the House debate that followed nowhere near approached the acrimonious arguments that greeted Jefferson's offer to sell his library to Congress, Lacey's proposal did not meet with immediate unanimous consent. When Lacey took to the House floor to defend the notion on May 10, 1902, he was surprised by pointed criticism even from his own party.[13]

A fellow Republican, Charles H. Grosvenor of Ohio, had apparently not heard the news of the book's discovery. When the Speaker of the House David B. Henderson announced the bill to be introduced, Grosvenor called out simply, "Mr. Speaker, what is this?"

"Congress has published all the works of Thomas Jefferson with the exception of this volume," Lacey responded, "and that was not published because it was not then in the Congressional Library."

Apparently dissatisfied with this response, Grosvenor asked again, "What is it?"

"*Morals of Jesus of Nazareth* as compiled by Thomas Jefferson," Lacey answered. "It makes a small volume, compiled textually from the four Gospels. This is a work of which there is only one copy in the world; and should it be lost, it would be a very great loss."

Grosvenor was not convinced. "Would the gentleman consent to put Dillingworth's spelling book as an appendix to the work?" he asked.

Dillingworth's spelling book was a perennial text used by school children throughout the nineteenth century. By 1901 it had the sense of an old and outdated tome, thus Grosvenor's indication here seems to be that if one was to print one text of a bygone time, why not another?

"That would be very amusing," Lacey replied, "but this is really one of the most remarkable contributions of Thomas Jefferson."

"Not more so than a great many other works of private enterprise by various individuals."

Perhaps trying to find a compromise between his partisan allies, another Republican congressman, Representative Sereno Payne of New York, interjected, "Why not substitute the four Gospels?"

"The Government owns this manuscript, and it is the only copy in the world," Lacey said.

"I wish it had never been found," Grosvenor retorted. While his objections seemed strenuous, he offered no further arguments, instead allowing Lacey to read into the record his appreciation of the book, and justification for its publication.

> Though it is a blue-penciled and expurgated New Testament, it has not been prepared in any irreverent spirit. The result is a consolidation of the beautiful, pure teachings of the Saviour in a compact form, mingled with only so much of narrative as a Virginia lawyer would hold to be credible in those matter-of-fact days . . . No greater practical test of the worth of the tenets of the Christian religion could be made than the publication of this condensation by Mr. Jefferson.
>
> . . .
>
> The jewels are taken from their settings, but they shine with their own luster. A verse of John is combined with a verse of Matthew with no interlineations, but is blended into a harmonious whole. In these days of

photolithography this little volume can be easily reproduced in facsimile. The work was intended to place the morals of Jesus in a form where, simple and alone, they could be contrasted with the teachings of the pagan philosophers. In doing this work Mr. Jefferson has builded better than he knew, and I trust that we may now have a reproduction of this beautiful volume in a form to be accessible to the Christian world.

The bill passed, but this was far from the end of the debate. Some members of Congress balked when they came to believe Lacey's intention was to produce an annotated version of Jefferson's redacted text. The possibility of framing a historical document with an element that might amount to government-sponsored biblical criticism was too much to bear for those who had been initially ambivalent.

Meanwhile, news that the US Government would soon be in the Bible-printing business had ignited both interest and alarm over Jefferson's religious ideas such as had not been seen in nearly a century. As it was reported in the Chicago *Inter Ocean*:

The so-called Jefferson Bible seems bound to make trouble. This is the more remarkable from the fact that it has been forgotten for nearly a century. In fact, the phrase, "innocuous desuetude," fits the past state of the volume as if it had been coined for it. So completely had the Jefferson Bible been forgotten that when the House of Representatives passed a resolution recently to print 9000 copies comparatively few of the present generation knew that such a book existed.[14]

Now that they had been reminded, many of that generation wondered why this book, interesting though it may be, should find publication at the public's expense eighty-two years after its creation. The loudest voices against the proposal were those who, in theory, might not mind further printings of words drawn exclusively from the New Testament. Christian ministers of all denominations spoke out against it. As the *Catholic Advance* of Wichita, Kansas, reported:

> Clergymen are criticising the action of the National House of Representatives in authorizing the publication as a document, in an edition of 9,000 copies of Thomas Jefferson's compilation, entitled "Life and Morals of Jesus of Nazareth," otherwise popularly known as "Jefferson's Bible." The Philadelphia Ledger's Washington correspondent, announcing the action of the House, says that "Jefferson regarded Christ as man of superlative goodness, but without claim to the supernatural character with which Christendom has for nearly 2000 years invested him." The proposed publication will have an introduction of about twenty-five pages by Dr. Cyrus Adler of the Smithsonian Institution, who is a prominent and scholarly member of the Jewish religion in this country. The fact that the House had authorized the publication of 9,000 copies of a book which has been described as "presenting a consolidation of the teachings of Christ, with only so much of the narrative as a Virginia lawyer would hold to be credible" and also said to be imbued with the free-thinking beliefs current in France and America in the beginning of the last century, seems to cause considerable surprise.[15]

One apparently surprised clergyman was Dr. Kerr Boyce Tupper of Philadelphia's First Baptist Church. Like many ministers, upon hearing the news of Lacey's resolution, he immediately took to his pulpit to condemn the Jefferson Bible. Yet in doing so he took a unique tack. Tupper argued that Congress had no business supporting such a publication, not because doing so breached the wall of separation between church and state, but because the US government was in fact a Christian government and should not abet such obviously un-Christian activities. For good measure, Tupper added that Jefferson's interpretation of Jesus was fundamentally wrong.

> Our public prints have announced far and wide the suggested project of our National Congress to publish nine thousand copies of Thomas Jefferson's Bible, from which has been eliminated the supernatural and everything that bears upon the deityhood of Christ.
>
> Mr. Jefferson, it is announced, regarded Christ only as a man of high character and superlative goodness, without claim to any supernatural character. What may the Christian pulpit say, what should it say touching this matter?
>
> Clearly two things by way of introduction: First, the reveration of the character of our Lord is revealed to no man through the organ of intellect alone—the only organ it would seem used by our great statesman in this investigation. The strongest appeals in the Scripture are never to logical faculties, but always to the spiritual consciousness. Second, it would be poor policy on the part of our government to lend hand and authority to the publication of a work such as before described.

Ours is confessedly and conspicuously a Christian government, and Jefferson's Bible, if rightly represented, is essentially an unchristian work. Jefferson may print his emasculated Bible, and the House of Representatives may publish it, but four hundred millions of the world's greatest and noblest spirits will look up to the Divine Son and love, adore and worship Him who as no other has presented to the world a miraculous incarnation, a spotless character, a transcendent teaching, majestic miracles, an atoning death, a glorious resurrection, a radiant ascension, a mediatorial Being, at the right hand of the throne of God.[16]

While pulpits resounded with the condemnation of individual preachers, religious periodicals (including the Dutch Reformed *Christian Intelligencer* of New York and the *Catholic Union and Times* of Buffalo) also voiced their concern, protesting the plan for publication in the name of their various constituencies. Within those groups, the prospect of the Jefferson Bible's publication exposed fault lines that pit minister against minister in every denomination. A meeting of the national Presbyterian Preacher's Association convened to draft a statement of formal protest became mired in so much disagreement that it was forced to declare it had to "obtain further information before officially condemning the statesman's annotated book." The group's proposed resolution would have declared the publication of *The Life and Morals of Jesus of Nazareth* "a direct, public and powerful attack on the Christian religion" but the lively debate that ensued created only further confusion.[17]

"I believe that a policy of silence on such questions is more effective than interference in controversies of this sort," Rev. Dr. Joseph Cochran declared. "We ministers should be extremely cautious in adopting resolutions. In a case like this we are likely to be led by false presumptions to say something one day that we would have to retract the next."

In reply, the Rev. I. L. Overman argued, "If the people cannot look to us for unflagging vigilance in opposing the assailants of God's Word, to whom can they turn?"

Others called for moderation. The Rev. Dr. J. Addison Henry made an appeal for pragmatism:

> I have heard that the Jefferson work does not contain a single derogatory word against the Christian religion. Let us remember that "he who is not against us is for us." This so-called revised bible may help us. It has been said by members of Congress that the publication of this work was simply a completion of the publication by Congress of the entire works of Thomas Jefferson.

Louder voices called to mind the very prejudices of Christendom which Jefferson most despised. Rev. Dr. John Peacock, for example, said:

> There is an almost general misapprehension regarding the opposition to the publication by Congress of this work. We who oppose it do so on the ground that even if the ideas of Jefferson were harmless the fact that the 150-page introduction to the work is by Cyrus Adler, a man whose hostility to Christianity is notorious, gives to the work the stamp of an anti-Christian publication.

Unstated but known by all, this reference to Adler's supposed "hostility to Christianity" meant nothing other than that he was a Jew. Fears that Adler would somehow exert an anti-Christian influence on the work were entirely unfounded, and comically exaggerated. The resolution calling for the book's publication mentioned that his introduction would be 25 pages, not 150. In the end, the introduction provided by Adler, now fully aware that critics would be eager to find fault, numbered all of thirteen pages and focused mainly on the volume's physical description and provenance. He took great care that none could point to his Jewish identity as a reason to oppose publication.

Yet some members of Jewish community saw the Congressional printing of *The Life and Morals* as problematic. The *Jewish Exponent* of Philadelphia published a protest declaration, and the *Jewish Comment* plainly stated that no matter the supposedly secular virtues of Jefferson's project, "This is not the affair of government in this country and every Jew should be on the alert to safeguard against such acts of unwisdom."[18]

In addition to anti-Semitic ministers and members of the Jewish community, opposition to the publication brought together other strange bedfellows. Among the most strident critics of the government's proposed Bible-printing project were not just ministers, but publishers as well. The *Richmond Dispatch* reported:

> The preachers generally oppose the publication of the "Bible" by the government, and so do the publishers, the latter wanting the job for themselves. They wish to secure the printing privilege for general sale. They are, therefore,

reinforcing the clergymen who are memorializing Congress to rescind its action regarding the printing of the nine thousand copies. The protests of the ministers, who are said to be afraid of an erroneous impression of Jefferson's treatise on Christianity, continue to pour in, and the enterprising publishers are "pushing the game along," in the language of the street. A member of the House Committee on Printing, who is a proponent of the scheme to take the printing of the "Bible" out of the hands of Congress, said that in his judgment a million copies of the book could be sold at one dollar each, so widespread has become the interest in the book.[19]

With both the publishing industry and the religious establishment agitating against Lacey's well-meaning endeavor, members of Congress suddenly were on the defensive regarding a bill none seems to have anticipated would be controversial. Like the third president before them, some felt the sting of having their religious commitments questioned.

"Mr. Jefferson has been unjustly criticized in regard to this very book, and in justice to him it should be made public," the Chairman of the House Committee on Printing, Representative Joel Heatwole of Minnesota, told the *Washington Post*. He claimed that the idea of publication initially had not been that of the Committee, but of "frequent requests . . . for the publication of the book, these requests coming largely from ministers of the Gospel on the one hand, and people interested in the memory of Thomas Jefferson on the other hand."[20]

Perhaps missing the point that many critics simply did not want government involved in the business of publishing religious books, Heatwole added, "No one that examines this little volume will rise from his perusal without having a loftier idea of the teachings of the Saviour."

Lacey, for his part, was astonished by the uproar. "There isn't even a semi-colon in it that is not found in the Bible," he said.[21] Though many complaints had reached his office, Lacey had also received requests for copies from preachers from all over the country. Ultimately, it was the former that proved impossible to ignore.

Within two weeks of introducing the bill and speaking eloquently on its behalf, Lacey introduced a resolution proposing to rescind its passage, and offering to pursue publication with private companies rather than the Government Printing Office. It seemed, for the moment, that the odd coalition of those opposed to the publication had won the day. As one celebratory article reported:

CONGRESSMEN THINK AGAIN.

"Jefferson's Bible" Will Not Be Printed at This Time.

Jefferson's Bible will not be printed by the government, at least not at this time. A resolution calling for the printing of a number of copies for public distribution was recently passed by the House, but so many protests have poured in upon congressmen from clergymen all over the country that a resolution has been adopted by the House requesting the Senate to return the bill calling for the printing. It is the desire of the House now to get possession of the original resolution for the purpose of killing it, as the congressmen realize that it is not popular, and they fear the political effect. The objection to the Jefferson Bible is based broadly on the ground that he was a free-thinker and omitted all reference to the resurrection.[22]

In the end, the storm passed and Lacey's bill to rescind approval of publication was never taken up by the House. Publication of *The Life and Morals of Jesus of Nazareth* by the US Government Printing Office was scheduled for 1904.

Discussion of a private printing of the Jefferson Bible proved prescient, however. Given the length of time required to carefully photograph each page of the leather-bound volume, enterprising commercial publishers who had watched public excitement build after both the 1895 and the 1900 discoveries saw an opportunity. The extracts Jefferson had chosen for his Bible were not a closely guarded secret, and so it was a fairly simple matter to merely gather the necessary texts, typeset them, and produce a book that most readers would find indistinguishable from the English text included in *The Life and Morals*.

This was the path taken by St. Louis Publisher N. D. Thompson. Even as Congress dithered over if and when they would move forward with printing the book, it was reported that Thompson "has printed what he claims is a correct copy of the English part of the original." He expected, it was further said, "to sell a vast number of these books, not because of their intrinsic merit; but because of the great amount of free advertising that the Jefferson Bible has received of late."[23]

Thompson was a man of humble origins in Kentucky who had transformed himself into something of a media mogul, publishing books by subscription and a variety of periodicals including religious, political, and farming journals. "Thompson is a practical man—eminently so," the

Louisville Courier Journal said in 1899. "He can see a flaw in a business proposition . . . clear through a brick house. He knows what his constituency demands, and he supplies it."[24]

So quickly did Thompson move to capitalize on Congressional uncertainty regarding *The Life and Morals* that he was able to mention the US government's apparent decision not to publish in his first advertisements. Despite the "storm of protest" calling for cancelation of that publication, he wrote, readers need not be concerned about the religious propriety of the book he now offered.

> The volume was prepared by Thomas Jefferson for his own use and with no hostile purpose whatever. It, when properly viewed, should Prove an aid, rather than a hindrance, to Christian teachings, for Jefferson has shown the moral greatness of Christ without recourse to miraculous aids. Every essential of true Christian doctrine' is retained in the extracts made, and there is nothing antireligious whatever.[25]

Thanks to Thompson's business sense, it was his edition, not the one advocated by Lacey and introduced by Adler that became the first book identified as *The Life and Morals of Jesus of Nazareth* available to readers. Remarkably, however, in his haste to beat the official government publication into print, Thompson made a small but significant mistake.

Compiling his text from the list of verses Jefferson had included in his volume, but having no access to the original, Thompson had no way of knowing that Jefferson often used only half of a given verse if he found it only partially acceptable. Such was the case of Matthew 12:15. In this section of the Gospel, Jesus shares a teaching about the Sabbath with the Pharisees, who plot to destroy him. The text that follows, as included by Jefferson is:

> But when Jesus knew it, he withdrew himself from thence; and great multitudes followed him.[26]

In Thompson's 1902 edition of *The Life and Morals*, however, the same line reads:

> But when Jesus knew it, he withdrew himself from thence; and great multitudes followed him, and he healed them all.[27]

Jefferson had intentionally cut away those last words, yet in the publisher's zeal to produce the first printing of the Jefferson Bible, he inadvertently kept them in. Thus a text whose reason-driven *raison d'etre* included the removal of every reference to healing by Jesus, here allows a miracle. With only three words, the portrait of Jesus so meticulously sculpted by Jefferson changed dramatically.

Just as famous misprints of the Bible have come to be known by such names as the "Wicked Bible," which inadvertently encouraged adultery, and the "Murderers' Bible," which accidentally called for the "killing" rather than the "filling" of children, Thompson's variant text of the Jefferson Bible has lived on in ways its publisher could never have foreseen. As it was the first typeset edition of *The Life and Morals* available, it supplied the text for at least one subsequent print edition (1975's *Thomas Jefferson's Life of Jesus, Bicentennial Edition*) and many of the proliferating digital editions now available online.

Through this accident alone, the US Government Printing Office edition was the first publication of the Jefferson

Bible as its creator intended, with no healing included. However, it was soon joined by competing editions, as other publishers saw in the scrapbook a highly marketable product.

Before 1904 was done, Philadelphia publisher David McKay produced a tiny "vest pocket edition" with the title *The Thomas Jefferson Bible, Being, as Entitled by Him, "The Life and Morals of Jesus of Nazareth, Extracted Textually from the Gospels of Matthew, Mark, Luke and John."* Curiously, this edition too seemed determined to insert supernatural elements that Jefferson had done without. Following the text itself, a "Valuable Appendix of Biblical Facts" carefully lists all the miracles Jesus performed in the unexpurgated Gospels.

Even in the official version of *The Life and Morals of Jesus of Nazareth*, the intriguing issue of variant texts can be found. While Congressman Lacey had done all that he could to insert his exploits into the story of the Jefferson Bible, Cyrus Adler showed that though he himself had played an equal part in its new popularity, he was content to keep out of the limelight of this unlikely publishing phenomenon. When the first copies of the edition published by Congress appeared, its title page read:

THE LIFE AND MORALS OF JESUS OF NAZARETH:

Extracted textually from the Gospels in
Greek, Latin, French, and English

by Thomas Jefferson

WITH AN INTRODUCTION
by Cyrus Adler

A bit abashed, Adler made sure that subsequent print runs would shorten the last line to simply "with an introduction." He was proud of the work he had done to bring the Jefferson Bible to the world, but in the intervening years he had perhaps learned that publishing a work of heretical scripture had risks all its own. Besides, he said, "I felt that Jesus Christ and Thomas Jefferson were sufficient names for one title-page."[28]

Social Engineering

The accusations made by some Christian clergymen that Cyrus Adler had intended to write a 150-page introduction to the published edition of *The Life and Morals of Jesus of Nazareth* or otherwise alter or annotate the text in objectionable ways were born of anti-Semitic tropes warning of behind-the-scenes Jewish control of media and government, and thankfully soon receded. Once it was seen how basically reverent and religiously innocuous the finished product was, and how light the editorial touch of the Smithsonian curator proved to be, the questions of who had discovered it and why it was published became footnotes in its interesting history.

Twenty years later, however, the editor of a new edition decided that an epic introduction and significant changes to the text were precisely what the Jefferson Bible needed. In the process, the definition of what constituted the book expanded dramatically, leaving both the effort and the intentions of its original creator behind.

Though an ordained Presbyterian minister who led churches in Pennsylvania and New Jersey, the Reverend Dr. Henry Jackson found his true vocation in mid-life when he encountered the then-new discipline of social engineering. A European concept that arrived in the United States early in the twentieth century, social engineering sought to understand human interactions as complex machines that might be tinkered with the way a technician would repair an engine. No matter if the machine in question was a community, a company, a nation, or modern society as a whole, social engineers believed they could grease the wheels of progress.

After several years working for the Federal Bureau of Education, Jackson launched the College of Social Engineering in Washington, DC, in 1923. "The purpose of the college," it was said at the time, "is the preparation not of 'specialists' but of 'generalists.' A Social Engineer will apply the fundamentals of social intelligence to the organization of community life, industry, civic affairs and social programs generally."[1] As founder and president, Jackson hired as lecturers such well-known figures of the day as Edward Bok, the longtime editor of *Ladies' Home Journal,* John Dewey, one of the fathers of functional psychology, and the novelist and playwright Zona Gale, who had recently become the first woman awarded the Pulitzer Prize for Drama.

To lead such luminaries, Jackson successfully put himself forward as the first of a new breed of problem solvers. Newspapers around the country touted the niche he was carving out in Washington: "Social Engineer is New Job Created to Relieve City Error"; a headline in Iowa read, "Dr. Henry E. Jackson First Of New Profession To Prescribe For Ills Of Municipality."[2]

A new type of professional man, the social engineer, is about to be introduced to the public. If you think of sociology, its problems of alleys, community centers, Industrial relations, and institutions, and then think of an engineer, a person who plans and constructs, you may have an idea of the new social engineer and his job.... He is called in by a city or county to point out the defects in its management and to suggest a way to correct these defects. He surveys the entire social organization, makes a written report, and leaves the community a practical working plan to be carried out.[3]

As part of his mission not only to train social engineers but also to further explain their goals to the American public, Jackson began publishing books viewing well-known literature through the lens of the discipline. His first such work, published in 1922, was *Robinson Crusoe, Social Engineer: How the Discovery of Robinson Crusoe Solves the Labor Problem and Opens the Path to Industrial Peace*. This initial work reinterpreted the adventure story of an Englishman stranded on a desert island for 28 years as a work of social philosophy, highlighting every individual's dependence upon society and their longing to remake it with whatever tools might be available. Far from just a children's story of an inventive castaway marooned in an exotic locale, Jackson wrote, "*Robinson Crusoe* challenges modern industry on the foundation of its structure and also offers the solution of its problem which, if operated, guarantees to open the path to permanent industrial peace."[4] If this has not yet been noted of the text, the author proposed, it is mainly because generations have had a well-formed but wholly inaccurate understanding of the book even before reading it. "In order to learn the true nature of familiar things," Jackson argued, "it is necessary to go through the process of unlearning the false. But to unlearn is a painful process, especially if the process runs counter to self-interest, or to childhood impressions."

Such was the motivation also of Jackson's next foray into the literature of social engineering: *Thomas Jefferson's Bible: Undiscovered Teachings of Jesus*, published by the New York firm of Boni and Liveright in 1923. Perhaps because Jackson was no mere literary critic but rather a true believer in the notion that any existing condition could be changed through the application of "the fundamentals of social intelligence," he was determined not just to publish *The Life and Morals of Jesus of Nazareth* as it had previously appeared, but to see it transformed.

He hoped openly that doing so would cause a stir. Even before his lengthy introduction, Jackson included in the book's front matter "A FRIENDLY WARNING":

> All who lack the spirit of adventure or the eagerness to learn what Jesus really talked about or the courage to discover that they do not know what they think they do — are hereby warned against the risk they run in reading Jefferson's exhibit of the teachings of Jesus and Weymouth's translation of them, as exposed in this book.
>
> —*The Editor. Washington, DC July 4, 1923*[5]

Though he invited controversy and any attention it might bring, Jackson also sought to preempt the kinds of criticisms that had nearly derailed the 1904 publication. He did so by making the case that the true subject of the Jefferson Bible was in fact neither Jefferson nor the Bible, but rather America itself, as seen through its primary ideal: freedom.

That a document whose subject is freedom should have been published by the United States Government is altogether fitting in view of its direct bearing on America's experiment in democracy. For a special purpose, to be presently stated, this Government document is reproduced in a new edition, but in a form to make its contents available for general use, and for use not as a curiosity, but as an instrument of social service.[6]

In preparing his edition, Jackson decided the primary texts Jefferson had used no longer answered the needs of the day. Jackson did away with the columns of multiple languages, using only the English text, which he offered without separating lines into verses, but placing it all in paragraph form. Moreover, and significantly, instead of the King James translation that formed the English language column of the original book, Jackson used the Weymouth New Testament. Also known as *The New Testament in Modern Speech* this was a translation into nineteenth-century English by the British Baptist schoolteacher Richard Francis Weymouth. Jackson's lengthy defense of this decision served not only as an aesthetic justification but as a statement of political purpose:

There may be some who will say that because the Weymouth translation is not the one which Jefferson used, therefore it is not Jefferson's Bible. He used the King James version. Those who cannot distinguish between the substance and the form of truth think that if the form is changed, the substance is lost. The argument proves too much. For, if the form is essential, we should use only the language in which the teachings of Jesus were originally recorded, that is, the Greek. But it so happens that the American people do not speak Greek. We are, therefore, compelled to use a translation and, in selecting one, we should use the best for our purpose, that is, one which most accurately and effectively expresses the thought. Our purpose is to exhibit what Jefferson believed to be the teaching of Jesus. The King James Version has become stereotyped and worn smooth, like an old coin, whose imprint is obscured by excessive use. The tendency to keep religion cloistered, isolated, and harmless is an illustration of the process everywhere in operation towards crystallization.

. . .

To democratize religion, to put it to work in the market-place, to use methods for its progressive realization—this has always been a need, but its capital importance is today freshly discovered. A minor but necessary item in the process of democratizing religion is to take the teachings of one of the world's greatest experts in religion, and put them into the common speech of the people, print them in book form as any other book is printed, send it out to win its way as a comrade among other books, asking for no superstitious reverence, or, any other special favour, but only for a hearing on its merits. If we cannot practice the democratization of religion even to the slight extent of putting Jesus' principles into common speech, what hope is there that the principles themselves will play any effective part in the common life?[7]

That Jackson chose to use an entirely different text from the English rendition used by Jefferson is made all the more remarkable by the fact that Jefferson's original work was available to anyone who wished to study it as never before. Not only were there multiple distinct editions in print by then, a recent donation to the National Museum had provided a further view into the book's methodology. A 1920 Smithsonian report states:

> A very interesting supplement to the "Jefferson Bible" in the Museum's collection of Bibles is the addition of two English copies of the New Testament, printed in Philadelphia in 1804, from which Jefferson cut out the English version of "*The Life and Morals of Jesus of Nazareth*." These are the very copies to which Jefferson refers in a letter of January 29, 1804, to Doctor Priestley: "I had sent to Philadelphia to get two Testaments (Greek) of the same edition, and two English, with a design to cut out the morsels of morality and paste them on the leaves of book.[8]

They were also the very copies Adler had discovered in Baltimore more than thirty years before. A gift from the family of Joshua Cohen, the two New Testaments were united with the clippings taken from their pages for the first time in nearly a century. At the time Jackson was compiling his edition, the extant materials were there for the asking by scholars or even the merely curious. Yet Jackson had no interest in viewing Cohen's New Testaments, or even the original *Life and Morals* itself. The reason for this was remarkable: In his estimation, Jefferson had not created a Bible as Jeffersonian as he might have. And the translation was only the beginning of it.

Jackson insisted that certain parts of the New Testament which should have passed Jefferson's reason test, and thus ought to have been included, were unaccountably left out. In particular, Jackson pointed to the pronouncements he referred to in his introduction as "Jesus's inaugural address" as it appears in Luke 4:14–30. In many New Testament editions, this section is called "Jesus Rejected at Nazareth." Jackson gave it the more hopeful title of "Open Forum Discussion."

He came to Nazareth, where He had been brought up; and, as was His custom, He went to the synagogue on the Sabbath, and stood up to read. And there was handed to Him the book of the Prophet Isaiah, and, opening the book, He found the place where it was written, "The Spirit of the Lord is upon me, because He has anointed me to proclaim Good News to the poor; He has sent me to announce release to the prisoners of war and recovery of sight to the blind: to send away free those whom tyranny has crushed, to proclaim the year of acceptance with the Lord." And rolling up the book, He returned it to the attendant, and sat down—to speak. And the eyes of all in the synagogue were fixed on Him. Then He proceeded to say to them, "Today is this Scripture fulfilled in your hearing." And they all spoke well of Him, wondering at the sweet words of kindness which fell from His lips, while they asked one another, "Is not this Joseph's son?" "Doubtless," said He, "you will quote to me the proverb, 'Physician, cure yourself: all that we hear that you have done at Capernaum, do here also in your native place.'" "I tell you in solemn truth," He added, "that no

Prophet is welcomed among his own people." Then all in the synagogue, while listening to these words, were filled with fury. They rose, hurried Him outside the town, and brought Him to the brow of the hill on which their town was built, to throw Him down the cliff; but He passed through the midst of them and went His way.[9]

So important did Jackson find these verses to the very idea of the Jefferson Bible that he decided simply to add them back in, effectively returning to the scene of the crime and making a few more cuts to the mutilated New Testaments that had recently found their way to Washington. He justified it:

Why Jefferson omitted it is difficult to understand because no passage could have better exhibited the value of the principle he employed in the selection of his material. His plan was to include only those passages on which he could absolutely rely as statements of the principles and ideals of Jesus, separated from all doubtful and controversial matter. This principle of selection requires the inclusion of the address at Nazareth. Moreover, it pointedly serves Jefferson's aim.[10]

That aim, as the title of "inaugural address" suggests, was a melding of the ideals of the Gospels, as Jackson understood them, with the American ideals of the equality of opportunity and the betterment of society.

The meeting at Nazareth was an open forum and therefore a workingman like Jesus was permitted to make a speech. In stating the purpose of His mission and His program of action He discussed such subjects as poverty,

CHAPTER 6

war, ignorance, freedom from tyranny, and the cancellation of mortgages on homesteads. The speech was obviously designed to state Jesus' purpose of promoting a better social order, and its success was so pronounced that it broke up the meeting and caused serious disturbance, that almost ended in a tragedy. Why a passage so in harmony with Jefferson's purpose should have escaped his eye, cannot be explained as an oversight. It was not an accident. There must be a reason. The only explanation which seems to me to explain it is that Jefferson did not perceive that the passage fell within his purpose. Why did he fail to perceive this? The answer is highly illuminating on Jefferson's whole project of making a digest of Jesus' principles. Jefferson did not see that this address fitted his purpose, because it had been and still is, so obscured and distorted by layers of misinterpretation, that its meaning was completely hidden from him.[11]

In short, Jackson saw in the rejection of Jesus precedent for how Jefferson's contemporaries questioned his religious perspective. "While Jefferson's critics were contending and proving to their own satisfaction that he was an atheist, or at least an infidel," Jackson wrote, "they were totally unaware that this silent, lonely man in the White House was studiously working on the teachings of Jesus and devoutly reading them each night before retiring."[12]

If Jackson seems to have written with particular sensitivity about Jefferson's plight, it may be because he saw himself joined to Jesus and Jefferson in this suspicion and rejection. As an advocate of a new way of viewing the world and seeking its improvement, Jackson knew the sting of his contemporaries' skepticism. Jefferson and Jesus were of one mind about many things, the president of the College of Social Engineering insisted, including the fact that they too were social engineers.

> All books which concern themselves with the science of society treat the subject from one of three dominating points of view and, therefore, may be classified under one of three general captions, according as they consider things as they are, things as they ought to be, how to change things as they are into things as they ought to be.[13]

For Jackson, the Jefferson Bible was especially significant because "as a social engineer my business is to discover some efficient process for changing things as they are into things as they ought to be, and I can find it in no other document."[14]

While Jefferson himself highlighted the ways in which his thinking departed from the teachings of Jesus, Jackson saw the two as melded in purpose across eighteen centuries of history. Jackson suggested that if one were to hear in church a preacher propose that the ideas of Jesus could be found embedded in the preamble of the Declaration of Independence, the listeners would be shocked to hear such a claim made from the pulpit.

> Would it not at present be generally regarded as sacrilegious to suggest that Jesus and Jefferson had worked at the same task? And yet what is the simple fact, obvious to anyone from whom it has not been hidden by a smoke screen? Look at the preamble of the Declaration. The three basic rights which it treats—"life, liberty and the

pursuit of happiness"—are not these subjects exactly paralleled in the teaching and thought of Jesus? First—"life"; said Jesus, "I have come that they may have life and may have it in abundance." Second—"liberty"; said Jesus, "Ye shall know the truth and the truth will make you Free." Third—"the pursuit of happiness"; said Jesus, "I have spoken to you that my joy might remain in you and that your joy might be full." From the standpoint of undistorted facts, is it not obvious that these causes were common to Jesus and the author of the Declaration?[15]

For Jackson, Jefferson and Jesus were further joined by a call to action. Those who would follow them, Jackson insisted, must work to create "a mental revolution" in their generation, just as they had in their own. "To work a mental revolution is a slow process of education," he wrote. "How far we have to go before effecting such a mental revolution becomes obvious enough when we observe the prevailing custom in the field of social endeavor along almost any line."[16] As an example, Jackson shifted from the lofty rhetoric of ideals to the very practical matter of raising money for those in need.

One has no difficulty in getting almost any amount of money for almost any kind of thing except the thing that is fundamental and important. It is easily possible to secure large amounts of money to buy crutches for Johnny who broke his legs by falling over a precipice, but next to impossible to secure money to build a parapet on the precipice to prevent Johnny from crippling himself and needing crutches. The reason is, we do not see the precipice. We are short on social intelligence. As individuals we are quite clever—we have inventive genius, we have creative ability; but as a society we lack intelligence. The chief method we have devised as yet for making social progress is through a catastrophe.[17]

Just in case any of his readers might have been taken aback by this sudden turn to such mundane matters, Jackson insisted that is precisely the point.

Out of the one hundred sections of His teaching in the Jefferson Bible as many as fourteen are devoted to the practical question of money. He treated this disturbing question more than any other, and to a surprising extent. . . . Contrary to common opinion, Jesus was eminently practical; He was a poet, a maker, a builder, a social engineer. Our sole aim here is to discover whether Jesus offered a big constructive principle effective for the creation of a better society.[18]

Through his 129-page introduction, Jackson made an elaborate, detailed, and passionate case that indeed Jesus had done just that. Yet the "big constructive principle effective for the creation of a better society" found in the Gospels turned out to be surprisingly simple, just as Jefferson had thought it to be. Only the accretions of history—the "dross of his biographers"—had turned something pure and elemental into an unnecessarily complex theology supported by centuries of religious bureaucracy. The morals of Jesus, in Jackson's estimation, could be reduced to one word: duty.

The religion of Jesus, like that of every other man, was His attitude to life. What was His attitude to life? It was the attitude of duty, freely chosen without reservations

of any kind. Duty as a policy of social and political pro-
cedure, He offered as the transforming power to change
things as they are into something better. This is the ideal
that, He said, would create the new society, which to
Him was the *summum bonum,* worth living and dying
for. His first recorded utterance and His last referred to
it. To discover this ideal and maintain it against all opposition, He believed, is the commanding duty and satis-
fying joy for every man.[19]

A radical departure from previous presentations of *The
Life and Morals of Jesus of Nazareth*, Jackson's volume struck
a nerve among those readers it found. Even for those who
were generally opposed to the notion of vandalizing scripture for ideological purposes, *Thomas Jefferson's Bible* provided a new way of considering the contemporary relevance
of an ancient text.

One reviewer attempted to capture his surprise at what
Jackson intended and accomplished:

> Why is it, I am continually wondering, that religious
> books when they are authoritative and sincere, are almost
> invariably dull, and when they are popular, are almost in-
> variably vulgar? I have passed the last six months in mak-
> ing as complete a survey as possible of our current reli-
> gious literature, and the most I can say is that I am still
> alive to tell the tale.

Yet in reading Jackson's book the reviewer felt he had discovered one of those rare works which are "not only remarkable, but reek with human interest, and are as absorbing as
any thriller."[20]

Mr. Jackson, who is president of the College for Social Engineers and has written a number of books on social matters, has done a great piece of work in his introduction to the Thomas Jefferson Bible—a book, by the way, that has long existed and was printed by act of Congress, but which has been allowed to languish. Mr. Jackson uses the Weymouth translation and explains why . . .

While I do not at all agree with Jefferson, and to be candid, his method of remaking the New Testament to suit himself has shocked me, that is of no importance at all compared with the book itself, and with the lively remarks written about it by President Jackson. As a social document, it is extremely significant.[21]

Other readers agreed, and found *Thomas Jefferson's Bible* particularly significant for the ways in which it spoke to the moment at which it was published, in the shadow of war and, as we can know only now, in the calm before the storm of the Great Depression. As another reviewer wrote:

Nobody who is oppressed with the feeling that our institutions are out of adjustment with religion or that things are going wrong with the world and yearns to know the reason, should fail to read the first four explanatory chapters by the editor, Henry E. Jackson, a former clergyman and editor, and now a "social engineer."[22]

* * *

While reviews were enthusiastic, Jackson's interpretation of *The Life and Morals of Jesus of Nazareth* did not make quite the splash that he had hoped. Never did it garner the same kind of press attention or popular outcry that had greeted the editions published earlier in the century. Yet one legacy of his efforts can be seen in the work he continued to do until his death in 1939.

In the aftermath of the Great Depression, national conversation turned to that ideal Jackson found at the core of the Jefferson Bible: the responsibility individuals had to their nation, and the responsibility a nation had to individuals. Called to testify before Congress during the development of the Social Security Act of 1935, Jackson elaborated upon his understanding of "life, liberty and the pursuit of happiness," which a dozen years earlier he had proposed as a "common cause" that tied Jesus and Jefferson together.

> Strangely enough the right to work was not among the basic natural rights listed by Thomas Jefferson in the great declaration which gave birth to the Nation; only the rights to life, liberty, and the pursuit of happiness. But the right to the pursuit of happiness is merely theoretical and meaningless unless one has a right to the things which produce happiness; the right to liberty is theoretical and meaningless unless one is in a position to exercise it; the right even to life itself is theoretical and meaningless unless one has a right to secure the means necessary to support it. The right to work, to earn a living, to secure enough to support a family in decency, is a prior antecedent right, without which no other rights have value.[23]

Once again, Jackson found that Jefferson had not made a point the social engineer believed he should have. And once again, Jackson was happy to correct the record by adding some words of his own.

Congressional Inheritances

When Franklin Delano Roosevelt presided over the laying of the cornerstone for the Jefferson Memorial on November 15, 1939, among the items set beneath the foundations of the neoclassical edifice were two examples of the third president's legacy: the Declaration of Independence and the Jefferson Bible. As Roosevelt said that day:

> He lived, as we live, in the midst of a struggle between rule by the self-chosen individual or the self-appointed few and rule by the franchise and approval of the many. He believed, as we do, that the average opinion of mankind is in the long run superior to the dictates of the self-chosen. During all the years that have followed Thomas Jefferson, the United States has expanded his philosophy into a greater achievement of security of the nation, security of the individual, and national unity, than in any other part of the world.
>
> It may be that the conflict between the two forms of philosophy will continue for centuries to come; but we in the United States are more than ever satisfied with the republican form of Government based on regularly

recurring opportunities to our citizens to choose their leaders for themselves. Therefore, in memory of the many-sided Thomas Jefferson and in honor of the ever-present vitality of his type of Americanism, we lay the cornerstone of this shrine.[1]

In the years since the Jefferson Bible's rediscovery and the birth of its widespread popularity, "his type of Americanism" had come to be typified not just by the pen that produced "When in the course of human events" but also by the blade that carved a reason-tested portrait of Jesus out of the raw material of scripture.

But of course, it was not the original *The Life and Morals of Jesus of Nazareth* itself that was placed in the cornerstone of the monument. It was instead one of the nine thousand copies commissioned by Congress, not the first printed edition of Jefferson's redaction, but the one that had come to seem nearest to his efforts. Because the leather-bound scrapbook created at Monticello rarely left Washington (after its arrival it had traveled only to Atlanta in 1895 and to New York to be photographed in 1904), when the majority of Americans interacted with the Jefferson Bible it was with one of the many published editions available. Among these, the official Government Printing Office edition had pride of place. Ironically, those who owned a copy of this testament to Jefferson's "type of Americanism" usually belonged to the chosen few.

Though three thousand of the original nine thousand were set aside for use by the Senate, and six thousand were reserved for the House, it was not only members of Congress who were lucky enough to possess them. Immediately following printing, the offices of Congress were flooded with constituents' requests for copies, the granting of which was at the discretion of the elected officials. Some copies undoubtedly fell into the hands of those owed favors or with favors to bestow, others went on display at schools and libraries. As one article from the time suggests, the desire to possess these small pieces of recently unearthed history was near universal:

DEMAND

For the "Jefferson Bible"

Simply Appalling

Congressional secretaries are working overtime and conducting little perspiring sessions of their own, in acknowledging the unanimous demand of the great American public for "Jefferson Bibles." Every Senator and Representative has been held up many hundreds of times by clamoring constituents. The thirty-two copies of the popular volume allotted by Congress to each Senator, and the fifteen copies to each Representative, if multiplied by hundreds, would not satisfy the biblical rapacity of the nation. Everybody wants a Jefferson Bible . . .

But the "Jefferson Bible" is richly worth a scramble for. It is a chef d'oeuvre of the Government printing office and a thing of remarkable intrinsic as well as classic value. It is a shame there are not enough to go around . . .

Since the wonderful book is to be had, if had at all, only for the asking, like Patent Office reports and garden seeds, and other beneficences at the hands of your

Congressman, the deluge of applications for the Jefferson Bible is appalling. The poor overwhelmed "members" are breathing threatenings and slaughters against that malevolent advertiser in a recent magazine, who called attention to his breakfast food or his "$2.00 pants," by the startling question, "Have you seen the Jefferson Bible?" kindly informing you if you hadn't that the Congressman from your district would be tickled to death to send you one! Clergymen, college presidents, infidels, actresses, journalists, Gentiles and Jews, Cretes and Macedonians, are equally in the frenzied stampede after a Jefferson Bible. But everybody but fourteen of each Congressman's friends will have distress as their portion.

So if you haven't gotten your Jefferson Bible, gentle reader, you won't. Save your postage stamp, and content yourself with the Golden Text for next Sunday.[2]

The Congressionally approved publication of *The Life and Morals* in 1904 was a dropped rock that rippled across the twentieth century, resulting in every other published edition of the Jefferson Bible. For the most part the impetus provided by the initial printing was simply as inspiration. Yet the books created by that act of Congress have also had a more personal effect, particularly among the families of the congressmen who received them, and who treasured the volumes long after the men to whom they were presented had died. In two cases, those original editions, passed down from one generation of "self-appointed few" to the next, had a direct impact on the ongoing dissemination, interpretation, and transformation of Jefferson's work.

Not long after FDR presided over the laying of the Jefferson Memorial's foundation stone, the first edition of *The
Life and Morals of Jesus of Nazareth* since Henry Jackson's
appeared in bookstores. Published in New York by Wilfred
Funk, Inc. in 1940, this edition, for the first time, was simply
called *The Jefferson Bible*. The task of framing the text for
what would prove to be the most consequential decade of
the century fell to a man who might not have seemed suited
to the task.

Douglas Lurton began his career in publishing as a news-
paperman, and then spent many years editing lifestyle maga-
zines with titles like *Your Life*, *Women's Life*, *Your Health*,
and *Your Personality*, which garnered him a reputation as
"one of the most astute mag men in the biz," according to
Variety.[3] When Lurton made his way to books it was more
as a collector and collator than a writer. The very popular
volumes he was responsible for bringing into the world included *The Power of Positive Living* and *The Complete Home
Book of Money-Making Ideas*. A Bible scholar he was not.

Lurton had come to the book honestly, however. Though
he achieved great success in the book business, he did not
push for the publication of *The Life and Morals* merely as a
moneymaker. For him, the book was a connection to a family
legacy of service and piety, both of which he seems to have
had in lesser measure than his forebears. As he wrote in his
introduction to the 1940 edition, "One of the first copies of
the so-called Jefferson Bible issued by the government printing office was secured by my father through the good offices
of my grandfather, the late Congressman Clinton Babbitt."[4]

One Sunday while he was still very young, Lurton recalled, he pleaded with his father to read him a story. The

senior Lurton was a small-town schoolteacher who valued learning above all else. In response to the boy's request, his father told young Douglas he would read "the most beautiful story in the world." He then read aloud from the Jefferson Bible.

> He charged me to treasure it among all of the many hundreds of books in his schoolmaster's library. I did treasure it for even as a boy I was impressed by the simplicity of the volume as compared to the mellowed big Bible from which my soft-voiced mother frequently read aloud. Down through the years I have kept the Jefferson Bible with its readily accessible story of the life and morals of Jesus.

As it was for other descendants of congressmen who had been in office in 1904, the Government Printing Office edition signified not just a founding father, but actual fathers, who had been fortunate enough to be present when the book became available, and who had been forward thinking enough to recognize that their heirs may come to value it.

For Lurton, it was one of a pair of family Bibles that had animated his childhood. While his father's stood for paring tradition down to its essentials, his mother's Bible, in quite opposite fashion, was crammed full not only of the full text, "worn, copiously annotated and underscored," but also of poems and clippings she had found spiritually edifying. These two books together informed his interpretation of the Jefferson Bible, which Lurton found unambiguously to be a monument to Jefferson's religiosity. There is no indication in his introduction that Jefferson had harsh words for the intelligence of the evangelists and the intentions of others whom he believed had distorted Jesus through the years. Instead, the book is presented merely as a work of compression, which had resulted in "the most exquisite story ever written."

Referring to the two Bibles that connected him to his parents in order to explain his desire to publish *The Life and Morals of Jesus of Nazareth*, Lurton wrote:

> I kept these matchless volumes, turning to the one with all of its sentiment and to the other with its rare clarity and simplicity, dreaming the while that the Jefferson Bible should be given the one thing it lacks—the beauty and legibility made possible by modern typography, and release from the obscurity of the national museum and collectors' shelves.

Lurton did not mention that there had been other editions offered in modern typography by then, or that the Jefferson Bible had not lain in obscurity at the Smithsonian in generations. It was a book that was always being rescued from forgetting, pulled into the light, uncovered like a buried treasure, which for the publisher it turned out to be.

It did well especially for Lurton himself. Several more editions appeared throughout the decade that followed. Some had different titles, such as *Life Sayings and Words of Jesus, Selected and Arranged by Thomas Jefferson*, but all made use of Lurton's introduction, sharing the story of his family's connection to the book under a variety of covers. Lurton's Jefferson Bible turned out to be so successful, in fact, that he soon published *My Mother's Bible: A Scrapbook Treasury of Verse and Wisdom*, a collection of the poems and clippings his mother had included in the other sacred volume that had defined his youth.[5]

What both these books had in common, other than their significant place in one man's life, was the reassurance they seemed to offer in time of impending war. The full text of Lurton's edition of *The Jefferson Bible* was published in serial form in December 1940, along with an editorial framing it less as a work of history than of current events: "How timely that this little book comes to us at this hour, bringing, as a contrast to the anti-Christian butchery by the despots of the Old World, the inspiration of the life and morals of Jesus of Nazareth compiled by the father of American democracy."[6]

When the United States entered World War II a year later, interest in the book only intensified, and seemed to build with hope for the war's resolution. As the *Dayton Daily News* opined:

> The world moves closer with time to Thomas Jefferson the man so far ahead. Men strive to earn such freedom as he bespoke for them. The freedom which he sought Jefferson found sustained by the faith and conduct taught in his little book. The whole world had that book. How little use it made of it! . . . The world welters in blood, product of the greed, the lust for power, the love of glory, the brooding ill will which the teachings of the Jefferson Bible put at the root of all men's ills. So nearly one are the democracy of Jefferson and the faith and words to make "the most sublime edifice of morality which had ever been exhibited to man!" We celebrate just now in a world of woe the author of those sublime precepts. To such tragical effect have they been ignored.[7]

Speaking to the needs of the day in ways even its savvy editor likely found surprising, Lurton's edition of *The Life and Morals* proved to be the most popular of many competitors through the decades that followed. Republished again and again under various imprints, it was not supplanted until the 1980s, when another writer with family connections to Congress similarly detailed the genealogy of his attachment to the Jefferson Bible, finding in the passage of a book from a father's hands to a son's a life changing moment of communication and inheritance.

"In 1956, my father, Frank Church, won election to the United States Senate," Forrest Church wrote on the first page of the Beacon Press edition of 1989. "As had been the custom since 1904, on the day of his swearing in he was presented with a copy of Thomas Jefferson's Bible, *The Life and Morals of Jesus of Nazareth*. Two years later he gave the book to me."[8]

As it had for Lurton, the gift of this book that had first been somewhat ritually bestowed upon a member of Congress melded the political and historical with the personal and familial. Far more so for Church, however, it was also turning point in a life that might have progressed far differently. By the time he came to write his introduction to the Jefferson Bible, Church was a Unitarian minister with a Harvard graduate degree in divinity. Yet he had been raised by a lapsed Catholic father and a "lukewarm" Protestant mother in an "ethical-humanist home," as he described it, that was a bulwark not of any particular faith but rather of the Democratic Party. The book his father put in his hands thus came as a shock to his system.

On first reading, even to the eyes of a ten year old boy, Jefferson's Bible struck with the force of unexpected revelation. For instance, there was no mention of the virgin birth or resurrection. From my occasional bouts of Sunday school, I knew how the Jesus story was supposed to begin (with angelic visitations and an immaculate conception), and end (the empty tomb and ascension to heaven). Being skeptical by nature and upbringing, such miracles figured prominently in my resistance to this great story's saving power. Jefferson's *Life and Morals of Jesus of Nazareth* began to change all that.[9]

"Intellectual curiosity, not Christian devotion, drew Forrest to the Jefferson Bible," his biographer Dan Cryer wrote.[10] Yet initially young Forrest did not have the kind of intellectual curiosity that took him to school, but rather the kind that often kept him from it. He was in fact skipping school one day when he began creating a *Life and Morals* of his own, going through another copy of the Bible with a highlighter, marking the verses Jefferson had selected, as if shining new light on a book that previously had seemed to him filled with darkness. "It was like a game, a puzzle, and it was fascinating to me," he said. "But its half-life was very short in terms of gripping my consciousness. Whether a seed was planted then that was on a slow gestation . . . I don't know."[11]

Even after being introduced to the Jefferson Bible, Church's interest in religion was spotty at best, and in general took a back seat to more pressing matters for the average American senator's teenage son that he was. "Forrest picked up stray bits of Bible lore at Sunday school from time to time," Cryer noted. However, "his occasional forays to a Presbyterian youth group . . . are best defined as expeditions to scope out girls."[12]

It would take the coming of the Vietnam War for the first shoots from the seed of his interest to emerge. Graduating from Stanford University in 1970, Church knew he was highly likely to be drafted into the army. After a claim of conscientious objector status seemed unlikely to be successful, his mind turned back to the early questions that he had become engaged by while exploring the Jefferson Bible. Church decided to go to divinity school after college mainly to avoid the draft, but he also did so with an intention to return seriously to that book that had been so formative in his younger years, the book that his father gave him, and the one that they still had in common as their politics diverged, as they did within so many families during that volatile time.

Church wrote his Master's thesis on *The Life and Morals of Jesus of Nazareth* at Harvard Divinity School in 1974. Less a work of theology than of history, Church's argument was that Jefferson had produced a portrait of Jesus scaled to "the dimensions of a rational eighteenth-century man." In this, Church found that Jefferson's quest was not for the historical Jesus but for the "intelligible Jesus," a Christ of reason rather than of redemption.[13]

Yet, while many earlier published versions of the Jefferson Bible sought to convert the text to a less radical reevaluation of the Christian tradition than it truly is, Church, remarkably, was himself converted by his encounter with the words Jefferson chose. Church's graduate work on Jefferson, and the influence upon Jeffersonian thought by men like the Unitarian minister Joseph Priestley, led Church into

Unitarian Universalist ministry himself. Beginning in 1978, he served as pastor for more than three decades at New York's affluent and influential Church of All Souls on the Upper West Side. As his biographer Dan Cryer said of Church upon his death in 2009:

> In the '80s and '90s, he was a key national spokesman challenging what he depicted as the religious right's hijacking of flag, family and Bible. He was an eloquent public speaker and commentator on radio and television who also wrote books of enormous spiritual power and who, as a historian, showed great insight into the nuances of church-state relations in American history.[14]

In Church's own estimation, none of this would have been possible without his early introduction to the Jefferson Bible. And thus he presented his history with it as a kind of conversion narrative. Of Jefferson's redaction, Church claimed, "His Bible unlocked the Scriptures for me, opening up a whole new world, one I have been exploring with deepening wonder ever since."[15]

As significantly, Church remembered it also as the book that transformed his relationship with his father, fostering in the young man a new level of maturity that simultaneously allowed him to reinterpret a faith he had previously rejected.

> When my father gave me Thomas Jefferson's Bible he quoted a famous passage from one of Jefferson's letters: "It is in our lives and not our words that our religion must be read." This led to our first serious discussion of religion. It was also the first time religion made any sense

to me ... With the gift of Jefferson's Bible, a door opened to me that ultimately led to a vocation in religion.[16]

Church's introduction to the 1989 edition of *The Jefferson Bible* does more than any other to ground Jefferson's work in American religious history. True to his training as a Unitarian minister, Church saw this influence most of all. As he rightly noted, Jefferson himself had predicted that "there is not a young man now living in the U.S. who will not die a Unitarian."[17] Off base though this prophecy now seems, it does shed further light on the kind of country in which Jefferson might have allowed himself to imagine, one where his edited scripture might have proved most useful.

Yet as convincing as Church is regarding the debt the text itself owes to the Unitarian movement, his life and work speak also to the complicated legacy of all those Congressionally printed Jefferson Bibles finding their way into unsuspecting hands. As those nine thousand books passed down through the generations, there was no telling what readers might make of what they found.

As of this writing, copies of the 1904 edition for sale on eBay go for around $400; one inscribed as a gift from Representative James H. Davidson of Wisconsin lists for $871.50. Even as the text evolves and is reinterpreted to speak anew to every generation, there remains a premium placed on objects which seem all the more rare the closer they come to the original, even when the original is made up only of the commonest of parts.

Jefferson, Jesus, and the Sixties

As the pastor of New York City's Community Church through the middle of the twentieth century, Reverend Donald Harrington sought to keep his Unitarian Universalist congregation relevant during changing times. In 1960, the church began allowing the members of the newly formed Metropolitan Synagogue to meet in its sanctuary, an arrangement that continued for decades. Inspired by this successful interfaith collaboration, Harrington soon started to incorporate lessons from a variety of religious traditions into the church's services.

"The purpose and the program of the Community Church," one press report said, was to be an emphatically pluralistic house of worship, "which takes note each year of the major festivals and customs of the world's great religions, such as Buddhism, Hinduism, and Islam, as well as Judaism and Christianity."[1]

Harrington's efforts did not stop with religious diversity. For a time, his sermons were heard throughout the city, broadcast by WQXR, which was then the radio station of the *New York Times*. Straddling the wall of separation between church and state, he also became active in politics and was even once a candidate for lieutenant governor, on a ticket with Franklin Roosevelt Jr. As the *Times* later summed up his career, Harrington was "an apostle of liberalism from the pulpit of the interfaith, interracial congregation he helped build."[2]

When the New York publisher Clarkson N. Potter began planning a new edition of the Jefferson Bible for publication in early 1964, Harrington was a natural choice to provide an introduction. Founded just four years before, the publisher had already carved out a niche for itself by focusing on "high quality hardbound books, mostly non-fiction in the upper price range." It specialized in "books on Americana, science, the arts, and the contemporary scene."[3] With the proper framing, the Jefferson Bible could check all these boxes, and Harrington seemed the right person for the job.

At the time, Harrington was also writing a book called *Religion in the Age of Science*, and so was particularly well attuned to the Enlightenment-inspired questions that had motivated men like Joseph Priestley and Thomas Jefferson. This might have provided Harrington's primary perspective for interpreting Jefferson's redacted text, but as it happened the timing of the publication brought a new set of concerns to the fore.

On October 14, 1962, an American U-2 spy plane took high altitude photographs of Soviet SS-4 ballistic missiles near San Cristobal, Cuba, less than three hundred miles from Miami. The missiles' range of over 1,500 miles meant that American cities as distant as Chicago and Boston were suddenly at risk. When President Kennedy was informed of this threat two days later, the danger of open and possibly nuclear conflict between the United States and the Soviet

Union increased more quickly and dramatically than it had ever before during the Cold War. The thirteen-day crisis that followed terrified the nation and, along with the many other horrors of the 1960s, defined the era.

In such a fraught time, Harrington saw in the Jefferson Bible an unlikely blueprint for peace.[4] "As a counterbalance to the fears and follies of this age," he wrote, "we need the strong and simple faith of the Jefferson Jesus. As an antidote to the panic around us, we need to drink deeply of the peace found in his righteousness."[5]

This was likely not exactly what Clarkson N. Potter, the founder of the eponymous publishing house, had it mind when he decided to publish a new edition of Jefferson's *Life and Morals*. To be sure, any newly launched publishing venture with an interest in Americana might look to the Jefferson Bible as a good business decision. It was, after all, fairly cheap to produce. With the exception of the new introduction, it had no author to pay. The text was in the public domain, and the photographic plates of the original Government Printing Office edition were readily replicable. And though religion was not named among the publisher's stated concentrations, anyone in publishing at the time would been aware that they were in the midst of what some observers called a "Bible Boom."

"This is a great time to buy a Bible, with an unusually large variety of editions, translations and prices available," the *Des Moines Tribune* announced in 1962. Late that year, the Christian publisher Thomas Nelson & Sons' ten-year lock on exclusive rights to publish the Revised Standard Version of the Bible had come to an end, and immediately five other publishers jumped into the mix. Additionally, there continued to be dozens of readily available King James versions, as well as 1961's New English Bible and the recently completed Catholic translation by Monsignor Ronald Knox, whose publisher claimed he was the first person since Saint Jerome "to translate the entire Bible single-handedly."[6] (Luther's Bible apparently didn't count.) The market was then so crowded that the scholar of American religion Martin Marty took to the pages of *Christian Century* to narrow the field, cautioning readers against buying illustrated editions, which were mostly "sleeked up Nordic Victorian commercializations." [7] And then of course there was the Jefferson Bible. As the *Tribune* enthused:

> Even the freethinkers are not left out of the Bible boom. The Jefferson Bible has been available in a 50-cent paperback since December 1961. This is Thomas Jefferson's famous scissors-and-paste job on the four Gospels only . . . put together into a single narrative. . . . Jefferson left out everything that seemed to him "ambiguous or controversial" and "every statement of fact that would have been admitted as evidence in a court of justice." As Jefferson was a Deist and a skeptic, his principles of editing meant leaving out all the miracles, including the resurrection.[8]

The mass-market availability of *The Life and Morals* spoke to its wide appeal, but not necessarily to widespread understanding of the intentions of its creator. The article continued:

> The Jefferson Bible, oddly enough, is prominently on display in the conservative Patrick Henry Book Shop in Des Moines, along with McGuffey and Goldwater.[9]

The placement was not at all as odd as it may have seemed. The 1961 edition mentioned makes use of the same framing as the 1904 pocket edition which highlighted Jefferson's religious bona fides ("Thomas Jefferson was from early life a close student of the Bible," its introduction begins) while downplaying the heretical turn he took later in life. [10] This impression is bolstered by the choice of its illustrations: woodcuts reprinted from a sixteenth-century psalter. Remarkably, the images included more than once depict scenes Jefferson chose to omit: the adoration of the infant Jesus in the manger, tableaux of healing, even of raising Lazarus from the dead. If one only read the text casually, as was perhaps the most common way of reading it, one might come away with the impression that Jefferson believed in all those things the pictures showed. It was thus no wonder that a conservative bookstore would put such an edition on display.

Nor was it all that surprising that the Jefferson Bible would have found some strange bedfellows. The framing of *The Life and Morals* until then had been consistently counter to Jefferson's radical vision. In the public imagination, it had become unambiguously an affirmation of the religiosity of the founding fathers.

This could be seen with particular clarity when Jefferson was enlisted in commentary surrounding political and religious controversies of the day. In a series of court cases throughout the early 1960s, the question of prayer and Bible reading in public schools captured newspaper headlines across the country.

In 1962, when the New York State Board of regents authorized a supposedly non-sectarian prayer to be used at the start of each school day, challenges to the prayer resulted ultimately in the US Supreme Court case *Engel v. Vitale*, which found such state-sponsored prayers to be unconstitutional. The following year, *Schempp v. the School District of Abington Township* challenged a Pennsylvania law requiring the reading of Bible verses, while *Murray v. Curlett* did the same for the schools in Baltimore, Maryland. Issuing a joint ruling on both cases, the Court agreed that prescribed Bible reading in public schools, even if not mandatory, violated the Establishment Clause of the First Amendment.

Writing in December 1963, syndicated columnist Russell Kirk lamented that the Court's meddling was sure to create "Dreary Secularized Schools":

> What is the most scandalous act your child can commit in school? Smash the windows? Curse the teacher? Oh, no—such little diversions are taken for granted, in a good many school districts. The really shocking act is to pray. Since Chief Justice Warren and his colleagues decided that it was unlawful to pray and read the Bible in public schools, widespread defiance or evasion of these curious decisions has arisen, all across the country. Many school board officers feel that if children were entitled to pray in school from the election of President Washington until the election of President Kennedy, it is scarcely logical that piety should become unconstitutional, without legislative act or Constitutional amendment, all of a sudden . . .
>
> Even Thomas Jefferson, who was the author (in a private letter) of that celebrated phrase "a wall of separation between church and state," probably would have been

astonished and disturbed at the Supreme Court's decisions and their consequences. For in the plan of public
schooling which Jefferson drew up for his state of Virginia, both prayer and Bible-reading were mandatory. If
schools cannot even mention God and the moral order,
what of importance can they teach?[11]

Other commentators pointed out that, indeed, Jefferson
was so much an advocate for the Bible, he had even carefully
crafted his own compilation of scripture. Baptist preacher
Clarence Shirley Donnelly wrote in his "Yesterday and
Today" column in West Virginia's *Beckley Post-Herald*:

> While all the to-do is going on about having the Bible
> read and the Lord's Prayer said in the public schools,
> there has come to mind the story of the Jefferson Bible.
> Thomas Jefferson was the author of the Statute for Reli-
> gious Freedom in Virginia. Also this remarkable man
> had much to do with framing that part of the Bill of
> Rights granting freedom of religion to all Americans.
> Our third president made his own Bible.[12]

Still others saw in the Jefferson Bible a possible middle
path between those in favor of the religion in schools and
those opposed. As a letter to the editor sent to the *Tampa
Tribune* in December 1963 expressed it, reading *The Life and
Morals of Jesus of Nazareth* might satisfy all sides of the issue.

> In all the discussion of Bible reading in the schools that I
> have read in the papers, I have not yet seen any comment
> on which Bible is concerned. Obviously in most schools
> it would not be Theodore de Beza's Latin version of the
> New Testament scriptures. And certainly very few schools

could afford a Gutenberg. Perhaps a few might choose a Douay translation, but in general it would probably be one of the more recent revisions of a translation made originally in England. The Old Testament might well be read as history, if proper commentary accompanies the selections read. In all probability some sections would not be considered proper for school children. . . . If the reading is to be considered ethical education rather than history and myth, Thomas Jefferson's Bible might well be chosen. This is now available in paperback; as everybody probably knows, this consists of the sayings of Jesus only. If the reading is to be taken seriously, it should perhaps be incorporated into a regular course in the history of religions. Such a course would go far toward freeing the oncoming generation from the prejudices and misunderstandings still prevalent among old people.[13]

Published four months before the 1964 edition, this letter would have been encouraging to the book's publisher, for it captured precisely what Reverend Harrington set out to do: to reframe the Jefferson Bible as a document not strictly of the past but of the present and the future.

In keeping with the interfaith philosophy with which he had transformed his New York church, Harrington's edition begins with a seldom-used Jefferson quote as an epigraph:

Were I to be the founder of a new sect, I would call them Apiarians and, after the example of the bee, advise them to extract the honey of every sect.[14]

Much as Harrington had opened his sanctuary to celebrations of Diwali, Passover, and the Buddha's birthday, he opened his version of *The Life and Morals* to an understanding of Jefferson that was beyond the usual binaries of Christian or Deist, Devout or Infidel. In order to make sense of the Jefferson Bible, Harrington argued, one needed to think of it as simply one flower among many; "extracts"—the very word Jefferson used for his Bible clippings—taking some of its essence, leaving the rest behind.

From that opening gambit, the 1964 edition goes the furthest in producing a volume that is most like a Bible, at least in terms of being a compilation of various parts distinct in tone and intent. It provides a prologue by Harrington, then the full text in English in a readable form, then a full facsimile, and, finally, a full section of "Jefferson's Commentaries." Many other editions also include an appendix of Jefferson's correspondence related to his Bible redaction projects, but this one goes further by providing excerpts from 32 letters, many joined together by the editors with new titles, as if they were essays written by Jefferson himself.

But the true innovation of this edition of the text is to be found in Harrington's passionate introduction. Unlike the 1961 edition or those published a generation before, Harrington foregrounded not Jefferson's conventional religious upbringing and attachment to the Bible, but rather his deep ambivalence about being part of a religious tradition whose moral teachings he treasured but whose dogmas he could not fully embrace.

> From the time he was a young man, Jefferson had held unorthodox views about Jesus. He found himself, as a man dedicated to reason and interested in science, unable to believe the miracle stories and supernaturalism of

the New Testament, but nonetheless drawn towards Jesus, the man and moralist, the spiritual leader and social reformer. He found the stories and legends of the Four Gospels confused and confusing and longed for a simplified, consolidated version which would eliminate repetitive and mythological material and emphasize the simple, ethical teachings of the Master.[15]

Harrington identified with Jefferson's desire to sort the diamonds from the dross within the New Testament, and he went further still by arguing that the Gospels presented a choice that everyone who might consider themselves a follower of Jesus must make.

It has been said that there are two contradictory religions side by side in the standard New Testament—the gospel *about* Jesus and the gospel *of* Jesus. Jefferson was not interested in the gospel about Jesus, which he found false, misleading and impossible for an educated man to believe. He was passionately devoted to the gospel of Jesus, which stirred him to the depths of his being and was the most powerful motive force in his life.

This choice was not merely one relevant in bygone days, but rather one of vital interest at a time when society itself seemed to be at risk. Knowing Harrington likely wrote his introduction to the Jefferson Bible at a moment when the terror of the Cuban Missile Crisis had only recently passed, it becomes impossible not to detect the shadow of that crisis on every page.

Jesus lived in a time of calamity and crisis, like our own. It was an age of mass hysterias, of paralyzing fears, and raging expectations. Despairing men more and more turned to God to save them with miracles.[16]

As in Jesus's time, America in the 1960s was marked by a search for spiritual solutions, some novel, some based in tradition. Harrington used his words of introduction to speak to people of both ages, with Jefferson's text as a pivot in between.

They expected God to intervene in history with supernatural power and impose his kingdom upon men and earth. They were looking for a saviour to succor them without effort on their part. Jesus confronted them with a different concept. The Kingdom of God will not suddenly appear, lo, here, or there. The Kingdom of God is a divine potential within you. It grows where there is love. It spreads among those between whom there is good will. It encompasses the society where hatred is banished and brotherhood becomes the law of life. Its soil is the human spirit, its seed the divine potential in all men. Love one another, he said, as I have loved you and the Father will bless all with love.

The Jefferson Jesus is not precisely the Jesus that modern biblical scholarship might discover in the Gospels, but is infinitely closer to him than the Jesus the unaided lay reader is likely to discover in the standard New Testament. It is a Jesus in harmony with our present understanding of nature and human life and history, both a believable and an inspiring figure for us to follow. In these days when the Bible is rarely read with concern and care by lay people, the Jefferson Bible may help many to rediscover the beauty, simplicity, and power of the religion Jesus taught and lived. It is a pity that this literary treasure, Jefferson's bequest to his countrymen, should still, after so many years, remain largely unknown and unclaimed.[17]

A Christian minister, Harrington saw in *The Life and Morals of Jesus of Nazareth* an opportunity not just for the modern world, but also for the modern church. He believed the tradition of which he was a part had focused too long on talking about Jesus rather than acting as Jesus would. Far from an attack on Christianity, the Jefferson Bible was a new revelation with the potential to remake Christian churches in its image, providing a vision that was not merely corrective but transformative; it offered a path toward evolution that alone might save the faith from itself.

> This new edition of Jefferson's work comes at a time when Christian dogma is reeling under the impact of the scientific spirit. The religion *about* Jesus, with its otherworldly emphasis and its unnatural and unbelievable myths, is faltering. Sophisticated churchmen are being forced to acknowledge the mythological character of much of the New Testament material, but are urging their laymen to accept it *as myth*, without seeming to realize that myths may be legitimate and effective means of gaining insight into truth, but that myths cannot constitute our religion . . . Unless Christianity can now grow beyond the old religion about Jesus and rediscover the true religion of Jesus, it is bound more and more to lose its bound on the modern mind. Jefferson, almost one hundred and fifty years ago, saw this coming and

prepared for his own use *The Morals of Jesus*. His work might in our time be the means for saving many from the complete rejection of Christianity.[18]

Yet for Harrington all of this would be meaningless unless the immediate threat of nuclear destruction could be averted. Even for this, the Jefferson Bible offered hope.

This is a time also when the Christian spirit is faltering in the face of the massive terror of the atomic age and the great power conflict which, using weapons that science has put into men's hands, threaten to wipe man off the face of the earth. Fear is in the saddle instead of faith, and we are getting ready to hide ourselves in holes in the ground from the inferno of our own creation. Legitimate differences of opinion harden into hatred. Unassailable walls are built. Bridges are blown up. The die is cast towards disaster. Within this atmosphere, even the precious freedom for which Jefferson spent his life and which he believed to be an essential requirement of human nature and good society, withers and atrophies.

Jesus and Jefferson knew that fear is a vicious cycle that traps those who give way to it. Fear generates hate, hate provokes counterhate, which in turn creates more fear—until both fear and hate explode into war, in our time truly the war to end all war, for there will be no one left capable of fighting World War IV. The antidote to fear is love, the love that is both understanding and good will, both justice and compassion. Perfect love casts out fear because it can always find constructive things to do to resolve conflicts and dissolve enmities.[19]

Early in its publication history, there were many sermons made about the Jefferson Bible. As in Jefferson's lifetime, pulpits early in the twentieth century were filled with ministers decrying his infidelity and his blasphemy. Sixty years later, Reverend Harrington delivered perhaps the first sermon not *about* the Jefferson Bible but *of* it. *The Life and Morals* served for him as a text through which to see the world, diagnose its problems, and exhort his congregation to seek their resolution. It was a sermon delivered not in Harrington's interfaith, interracial congregation, or over the airwaves of a New York radio station, but in the usually staid pages of an introduction to a hardcover book.

> To overcome the deepening divisions which threaten our future, we need to build new bridges of imagination and understanding, reaching out from our side of the gulf which divides us, realizing that we can love our enemies without giving way to their injustice; we can help them with their problems even while we urge upon them new policies; we must be humble, recognizing our own failings and needs; we can accept in our own hearts the certainty that apart from a foundation of friendship with them there will be no future for anyone.
>
> Jesus believed that there is a seed of goodness in everyone, and that all our hope must be in appealing to that potential. He believed that *people* were all that matter, and that all men's institutions must be designed to serve human needs. It was this in Jesus that appealed to Jefferson, and led him to call Jesus the greatest moral teacher of the ages and the most powerful single influence in his own life.[20]

"It would be fitting," Harrington said in closing, "in this hour of gravest crisis and most desperate human need, for the Jefferson Jesus, the human Jesus, to have His say and day. Never has a generation needed his message more urgently than ours."[21]

Harrington's was not the last version of the Jefferson Bible published in the 1960s. Five years later, with the war in Vietnam raging and the wound of Martin Luther King Jr.'s and Robert Kennedy's assassinations still fresh, Eakins Press published a version of *The Life and Morals* it called *Thomas Jefferson's Human Jesus* late in in 1968. Following the most recent precedent, it also attempted to make *The Life and Morals* a book about now. It did so with remarkably spare framing. There is no introductory essay, only some limited copy on the jacket flap, which begins "In this little volume Jesus of Nazareth speaks to us as a man."[22]

The heavy lifting of presenting the book in contemporary terms is done on the book's back cover, which includes only two quotations. One from the recently martyred Dr. King:

Too often . . . men have responded to Christ emotionally, but they have not responded to his teachings morally. The notion of a personal savior who has died for us has a great deal of appeal, but too often Christians tend to see the Resurrected Christ, and ignore the man Jesus.

And the other from George Bernard Shaw:

Thus it is not disbelief that is dangerous in our society: it is belief. The moment it strikes you (as it may any day) that Christ is not the lifeless harmless image he has

hitherto been to you, but a rallying centre for revolutionary influences which all established States and Churches
fight, you must look to yourselves; for you have brought
the image to life; and the mob may not be able to bear
that horror.

There is a dichotomy established in both these quotations. On the one hand it is between the "man Jesus" and the
"Resurrected Christ," and on the other between "unbelief"
and "belief." In both cases it is the relevance and significance
of the first of each pair that is highlighted, a suggestion that
"Thomas Jefferson's Human Jesus" may indeed be the savior
called for by the times.

The change this suggests in the interpretation of the
Jefferson Bible is subtle but significant. No longer was it
merely either a secular experiment or a pious work of devotion; it was beginning to be seen as something new. It was in
itself a genuine religious expression, albeit not one orthodox
Christians were likely to endorse. Just as Jefferson saw himself as a Christian simply as one who followed the teachings
of Jesus, it was becoming possible in the 1960s to declare
oneself a Jeffersonian Christian, firm in the belief that one
understood Jesus and the Bible as Jefferson did.

The meaning and implications of the genuine religious
expression that the Jefferson Bible was becoming can be
seen in the statement of faith offered by another preacher
turned politician in the 1960s. Just around the time Harrington's edition of the Jefferson Bible was being published,
New York Congressman Adam Clayton Powell began to declare that his religious attitudes were "based entirely on the
so-called Jefferson Bible." Often criticized for his "fondness

for fine wines, expensive night clubs, fast cars and pretty women," Powell admitted that he might not be a typical Baptist preacher, but he found no rebuke in the text to which he most often turned for teachings in his faith. "I can't find anything in the sayings of Jesus against moderate drinking, dancing and card playing," Powell said in 1963. "But I do find a great deal that He said against hating and turning your back on your brother."[23]

As pastor of Harlem's Abyssian Baptist Church, Powell went further to claim *The Life and Morals* as a cornerstone of his community's faith:

We do not believe in the Bible as the word of God. It is too filled with contradictions. We believe in the Thomas Jefferson Bible. Carefully, that brilliant Founding Father cut from the New Testament only those words that Jesus spoke. Then in logical and chronological order, he put them together until he had created a new Bible, a new Bible of old words, only the words of Jesus himself. This is the Bible from which I preach.

For us God is a God of truth and that truth is absolute. Yet how can He contradict Himself? And the Bible is full of contradictions. I believe that the men who penned the words of the Bible were inspired, but all inspiration varies. Some inspiration does not reveal the final truth; some inspiration is so wrongfully received that no truth is revealed at all. Here and there as God speaks to man, as man becomes increasingly sensitive and aware of Him, man is privileged to be the recipient of the immortal flashes of the Absolute. Therefore, I believe that the Bible is still being written.[24]

While Jefferson might not have gone quite that far, he would have agreed that holy writ was a work in progress, in need of frequent amendment to respond to the needs of the times.

Choose Your Own Adventure

As the classically trained Jefferson would have known, the word *heresy* comes from the Greek *herein*, "to choose." In this, the Jefferson Bible is undoubtedly a heretical work, for it is nothing but a catalogue of choices made concerning the Gospels. As he turned through the pages of his various testaments, Jefferson faced countless forks in the road of the unified narrative he hoped to create: Which verses were believable and which were not? Which sounded like the man he revered and which like those who he believed had distorted his memory? Every time Jefferson put his penknife to the page, he chose to present one view of Jesus at the expense of another. Though he never hoped the book would find readers, down through the generations Jefferson effectively asked everyone who has encountered it to make choices of their own.

Two hundred years after those first editorial decisions were made, readers of *The Life and Morals of Jesus of Nazareth* remain divided on just how conventionally heretical—in terms of diverging from commonly shared Christian doctrines—Jefferson's work truly was. Some wish to believe it was much less so than it appears, that he produced "mutilated" copies of the New Testament, as Cyrus Adler put it, mainly for the sake of compression, simplification, and even evangelization. Others argue it was far more heretical than even Jefferson himself knew, that it was not merely a redaction of one set of texts made at a particular moment in an elder statesman's eventful life, but at once a key to unlocking all Jeffersonian thought, and a blade to be wielded against religion generally.

In the former camp, the leading figure in the twenty-first century has been David Barton, a self-taught historian and founder of the group Wall Builders, "an organization dedicated to presenting America's forgotten history and heroes, with an emphasis on the moral, religious, and constitutional foundation on which America was built."[1] Barton's book and DVD *America's Godly Heritage* has itself become a bible of sorts for a movement enthralled by the notion that the United States was explicitly founded as a Christian nation, and that it is a recent conspiracy to edit history that has obscured this fact.

A former principal of a Christian school in Texas, Barton's name first rose to national prominence with the help of high profile endorsements by the likes of former Arkansas governor Mike Huckabee who praised him as "the greatest living historian on the spiritual nature of America's early days," and former Minnesota Representative Michele Bachman who suggested Barton should give members of Congress lessons on Constitutional law.[2]

Barton's work is a useful reminder for those who needed it that there were indeed Christians present at the nation's founding; that the minds responsible for the documents upon which our nation is built knew their way around the

Bible; and that the cultural context in which the United States was born was indeed overwhelmingly Christian. Yet any attempt to argue, as Barton and other Christian nationalists do, that one religious perspective alone was the force behind the revolution and the creation of the republic quickly reveals itself to be less a blanket explanation than a quilt of disconnected events and quotations taken out of context, all stitched together with concern less for history than for the place of a certain type of Christianity in today's United States.

If one begins to pull at the threads of this quilt, it falls easily apart. For example: in *America's Godly Heritage,* Barton proposed that in recent years the Supreme Court has conspired to remove any trace of religious influence from the nation's founding principles. The court, he said, has even referred to itself, as "a national theology board."[3]

Is it possible a justice of the Supreme Court would ever say such a thing? Barton took the trouble to quote and footnote the phrase so the casual reader wouldn't have any cause to doubt it. Yet in the opinion in which the words "national theology board" occur, the statement is made by Justice Anthony Kennedy, who actually said: "The court is ill equipped to serve as a national theology board."[4]

Elsewhere, Barton often (and now somewhat infamously) quoted a letter from John Adams to Benjamin Rush stating that there could be no government without direct involvement of the divine: "There is no authority, civil or religious—there can be no legitimate government—but what is administered by this Holy Ghost."[5] Barton did not quote a line that follows, which refers to such claims as "Artifice and Cunning" which are believed only due to "the poor weak ignorant Dupe human Nature."[6]

Such selective quotation is the kind of sleight of hand one needs to perform in order to reduce the nation's religious heritage to a single story. It certainly did not seem like a single story at the time Adams wrote his letter. Given the folly of some religious views of governance, Adams thought it was no wonder that that Voltaire and Thomas Paine had won so many converts to the freethinkers' cause.[7]

In his 2012, book *The Jefferson Lies,* Barton took the same approach to the third president generally, and in one chapter to the Jefferson Bible specifically. As the book's publisher, Thomas Nelson—"a world leading provider of Christian content"—announced in a press release: "History books routinely teach that Jefferson was an anti-Christian secularist, rewriting the Bible to his liking, fathering a child with one of his slaves, and little more than another racist, bigoted colonist—but none of those claims are actually true."[8]

Organized around "seven contemporary claims about Jefferson's faith and morals," Barton's book proposed to debunk the "lies" Americans have come to believe about Jefferson by answering a series of questions: Did Jefferson really have a child by "his young slave girl," Sally Hemings? Did he found a secular university as a reflection of his own "allegedly secular" beliefs? Was Jefferson a racist? Did he hate the clergy? Did he repudiate religion? And, most relevant to our purposes here, "Did Jefferson write his own Bible, excluding the parts of Christianity with which he disagreed?"[9] To all these questions, Barton answered emphatically "No."

Leaving aside the appropriateness of this answer for the other questions, where the Bible query is concerned, it should be acknowledged that *no* is indeed the only correct answer to the question if Jefferson "wrote his own Bible." He did not "write" one, and the book he created is of course by no means truly a Bible. But without question Jefferson did edit and arrange verses from the Gospels to craft a unified account of the life and teachings of Jesus with which he could agree, and which would comport with the dictates of reason. No good faith reckoning with the book itself could lead to any other conclusion.

Yet one wonders if Barton did make a good faith reckoning with *The Life and Morals of Jesus of Nazareth*. His position rests on an argument that Jefferson could not have done what no one who has seen any edition of the Jefferson Bible is likely to claim. Barton writes:

> Logic would tell us that if Jefferson wrote his own Bible, he would do so only if we were thoroughly dissatisfied with the traditional Bible, especially its inclusion of the supernatural. Evidence definitively shows this was *not* Jefferson's view . . . Jefferson made frequent, positive use of Bible references and passages in his own writings.[10]

Though this last point is certainly true, the supposed evidence that he did not both make positive use of scripture and simultaneously find fault with the Bible leaves much to be desired. We are told Jefferson made donations to Bible societies, gave Bibles as gifts, and "owned many other full, uncut Bibles," but none of that changes the fact that he wrote at great length to trusted friends explaining what he had planned to do to the Gospels and why.[11] Jefferson took a blade to the New Testament to craft a presentation of its central figure closer to the ideals of the Enlightenment not despite his longstanding interest in the Bible, but because of it.

The project of *The Jefferson Lies* is not to make sense of Jefferson as a complicated individual, however, but to conscript him into the service of contemporary culture wars. On this battlefield *The Life and Morals of Jesus of Nazareth* can only be proof that Jefferson was a Christian as certain kinds of twenty-first century Americans interpret the term. The principal weapon in Barton's arsenal is selective quotation. In his hands, ellipses speak volumes. As he quoted Jefferson's 1813 letter to John Adams in support of his premise, it reads in part as follows:

> We must reduce our volume to the simple evangelists, select, even from them, the very words only of Jesus . . . there will be found remaining the most sublime and benevolent code of morals which has ever been offered to man.[12]

In the original letter, the words between "Jesus" and "there" are these:

> paring off the Amphibologisms into which they have been led by forgetting often, or not understanding, what had fallen from him, by giving their own misconceptions as his dicta, and expressing unintelligibly for others what they had not understood themselves.[13]

Barton scrupulously avoided any suggestion that Jefferson might have been "thoroughly dissatisfied" with a text he regarded as shaped by the forgetfulness, misunderstanding, misconceptions, and unintelligibility of the men who created it. Ironically, though through such elisions Barton misrepresented the stated purpose of *The Life and Morals*, his overall project is in fact not all that different from Jefferson's:

To remove those parts from a canon of writings that do not agree with a predetermined interpretation of its meaning. Jefferson redacted those parts of the Gospels which did not pass the test of reason, while in the Jefferson passage above and the Adams letter mentioned earlier, Barton redacted those parts of the founder's writings that might complicate the conclusion he hoped to reach.

Five months after it was published, the publisher Thomas Nelson recalled *The Jefferson Lies* because of widespread criticism of the liberties Barton took with the facts. After hearing from a number of scholars with concerns about the book, the publisher reviewed the text and admitted with chagrin, "in the course of our review [we] learned that there were some historical details included in the book that were not adequately supported."[14] As a Thomas Nelson executive told National Public Radio, "basic truths just were not there."[15]

Undaunted, Barton republished the book with WND Books, the publishing arm of World Net Daily, an online portal of right-leaning opinion and conspiracy theories. But for many in his evangelical religious milieu, the obvious and numerous errors in *The Jefferson Lies*, including Barton's mistreatment of *The Life and Morals of Jesus of Nazareth*, raised an important question about sources of knowledge and the inappropriate ways they can be weaponized in the nation's endless cultural skirmishes. As another evangelical online opinion portal, *The Gospel Coalition*, framed it: "Do we care about the truth, or do the conclusions we want to hear justify the means used to obtain them?"[16]

This could have been asked about the ways many editions of the Jefferson Bible have been presented, and it is worth noting that agenda-driven reframings of the book have not been limited to a single religious or political perspective.

Inspired by the fact that members of Congress for some fifty years received copies of *The Life and Morals of Jesus of Nazareth* from the 1904 Government Printing Office edition upon taking the oath of office, the American Humanist Association in 2012 made a new volume available for the same purpose. *A Jefferson Bible for the Twenty-First Century* presents Jefferson's redacted Gospels alongside excerpts of scripture from a variety of religious traditions. The then-director of the Humanist Press Luis Granados said:

> In 1901, the U.S. Congress felt that the Jefferson Bible was of such great value that it authorized the printing of nine thousand copies for itself. With today's Congress representing a much more religiously diverse population, including a fifth of the population that is not religious, we thought it was appropriate to deliver a new Jefferson Bible that acknowledges that diversity.[17]

That "new Jefferson Bible" included the full English text of Jefferson's effort, along with passages from the Hebrew Bible, the Bhagavad Gita, the Quran, various Buddhist scriptures, and the Book of Mormon. Whereas Jefferson had pasted only those Gospel passages he found reasonable into the blank book that would become *The Life and Morals of Jesus of Nazareth*, the American Humanist Association chose also to include many of the verses he left out, presented as "The Worst of the Gospels?" The tone is questioning to suggest both that such evaluations are subjective, and also to encourage debate. The electronic version of the book asks at the end of each section "Which passages would you like to see added to this list? Which would you like to see removed?" followed by an invitation to log onto the Humanist Press website to share opinions with other readers.[18] About the inclusion of the worst of the Gospels Granados wrote:

> This is not done to mock, but instead to reinforce the central point: the gospels are the work of well-intentioned but imperfect human beings, and should therefore be read critically, winnowing the good from the bad.[19]

While Jefferson might have disagreed about the "well-intentioned" nature of those he accused of "roguery" and "stupidity," he might have appreciated the book's stated goal of treating religious texts of all traditions with the same degree of scrutiny. "Humanists believe that religious scriptures, Christian and otherwise, are the works of human beings rather than anything supernatural, and as such contain a mix of good and bad ideas," Granados added. "That's one reason so many freethinkers strongly identify with Thomas Jefferson, even though they don't like everything he did."[20]

Yet the "best" and "worst" of other traditions don't always seem to have been chosen with the same rigor Jefferson applied when creating *The Life and Morals*. Among the choices for the Hebrew Bible, for example, we find listed as some of the "best" Genesis 13:8 ("And Abram said unto Lot, Let there be no strife, I pray thee, between me and thee, and between my herdmen and thy herdmen; for we be brethren."),[21] Exodus 22:22 ("Ye shall not afflict any widow, or fatherless child")[22] and Proverbs 10:7 ("The memory of the just is blessed: but the name of the wicked shall rot.")[23] All of these likely would have passed muster with Jefferson, but some of the supposed "worst" are puzzling. Included among that group is Deuteronomy 22:11 which states, "Though shalt not wear a garment of divers sorts, as of woollen and linen together."[24] To be sure, this is a strange prohibition to modern sensibilities, but is it among the "worst" passages in the Hebrew Bible?

Similar questions arise with the other scriptures included. At times, the intention of *A Jefferson Bible for the Twenty-First Century* seems to be merely to mine the world's religious traditions for pithy upbeat messages or inoffensive folk aphorisms with universal application, as when it includes Sura 94:6 as among the "best" of the Quran: "Verily, with every difficulty there is relief,"[25] or Dhammapada 63 as among the "best" of Buddhist scriptures: "The fool who knows his foolishness is at least wise so far; but a fool who thinks himself wise, he is called a fool indeed."[26] With quotability and accessibility as apparent qualifications for the "best," it is not surprising to find among the "worst" passages those that seem thoroughly inscrutable outside the context of a given tradition, as is the case when the Death of the Buddha from the Mahâ-Parinibbâna-Sutta is listed last among the "Worst of the Buddhist Sutras":

> Thereupon The Blessed One rising from the cessation of his perception and sensation, entered the realm of neither perception nor yet non-perception; and rising from the realm of neither perception nor yet non-perception, he entered the realm of nothingness; and rising from the realm of nothingness, he entered the realm of the infinity

of consciousness; and rising from the realm of the infinity of consciousness, he entered the realm of the infinity of space; and rising from the realm of the infinity of space, he entered the fourth trance; and rising from the fourth trance, he entered the third trance; and rising from the third trance, he entered the second trance; and rising from the second trance, he entered the first trance; and rising from the first trance, he entered the second trance; and rising from the second trance, he entered the third trance; and rising from the third trance, he entered the fourth trance; and rising from the fourth trance, immediately The Blessed One passed into Nirvana.[27]

Given that Jefferson did not include the Resurrection in his telling of the life of Jesus, it is plausible that he would have looked similarly askance at such an elaborate telling of the metaphysical circumstances of the Buddha's passage into Nirvana. Yet in this and other instances, the choices made by the editors of *A Jefferson Bible for the Twenty-First Century* are unpersuasive, not because Jefferson would not have agreed with many them, but because they push the notion of what a "Jefferson Bible" might be too far beyond its original context and intent.

While *A Jefferson Bible for the Twenty-First Century* does not gloss over or intentionally obscure relevant facts about Jefferson's biblical redaction project in the manner of David Barton, in its expansive view of the meaning of *The Life and Morals* it is in some ways as slanted in its interpretation as *The Jefferson Lies*. It proposes that the Jefferson Bible was less a limited project informed by the particulars of Jefferson's experiences, education, and environment, and more of a universally applicable methodology—that Jefferson's blade, in other words, would cut equally well through any sacred text. However, the circumstances that led Jefferson to edit the Gospels were so closely tied to the widespread engagement with Enlightenment ideas that occurred throughout his lifetime that the logic of applying his method to other traditions, born and developed in far different historical conditions, is inevitably strained.

Yet to greater and lesser degrees, this is what every edition of *The Life and Morals of Jesus of Nazareth* has done. With each new Jefferson Bible proving to be subtly different, each a product of editorial choices that naturally are entwined with scholarly fashions, shifting religious sensibilities, and the needs of the marketplace, it is a book that has evolved considerably during its two-hundred-year history, and will continue to do so.

The past dozen years have seen not only a proliferation of digital editions available for immediate download on the internet, but also those published, for the first time, in languages beyond the original four Jefferson employed.

Released in 2008, *Vida y doctrinas de Jesus* provides a Spanish translation of the text. An introduction by the Cuban-born poet Emilio de Armas recounts the usual narrative of its inspiration and production, but then goes further by positioning it with a discussion of the Renaissance theologian Migel Servet. In his sixteenth-century works, Servet rejected traditional conceptions of the Trinity, much as Jefferson did in his youth. The earlier philosopher paid for this rejection with his life, however. In 1553 he was burned at the stake in John Calvin's Geneva, made to hold in his arms volumes of his writing as the flames consumed him. Jefferson mentioned this execution more than once in his correspondence concerning thoughts on religion, and yet it was not until *The Life and Morals* appeared in Spanish that any edition connected this martyr to the cause of the freedom of conscience as one of the Jefferson Bible's possible inspirations.

A decade later, *Die Jefferson-Bibel, Der wahre Kern des Neuen Testaments* appeared in German. Three years before, Tobias Huch, a journalist who often writes about the refugee crisis in Europe and the Middle East, stumbled upon the text by accident. Upon first reading, he immediately discovered that it spoke both to his distrust of the notion of officially sanctioned religion and his belief that the essence of Christianity could be stated much more purely and simply than history had usually allowed.

> Especially young people are looking for clear, catchy, and convincing messages, often with a spiritual orientation. Through my political fight against the current advance of radical ideologies in our streets, it's well known to me that adolescents and young adults are looking for a value system. This value system must be attractive and above all else understandable. And unfortunately the Bible rarely offers that today; it is too extensive, too complex, too incomprehensible. . . . In the Jefferson Bible, I recognized the opportunity to give Christian values to young people.[28]

Just as *The Life and Morals of Jesus of Nazareth* has spoken to those who published it in the early 1900s, the 1920s, the 1940s, and the 1960s, today in the shadow of the latest wars, Huch saw something in the book whose appeal could not be more timely. Around the same time as he had discovered Jefferson's redaction of the Gospels, he noted, he was traveling on a humanitarian mission to the war zones of Iraq and Syria.

"I saw their incredible terror and suffering, which continue to plague me today," Huch wrote. "But reading and editing this timeless biblical text has helped me to get through all those terrible impressions unscathed."[29]

Jefferson could not have imagined the many purposes to which his private collection of New Testament verses would be put, but the spirit of the original book remains in every successive iteration. Today more readers than ever before are able to take up Jefferson's heretical text. They are variously enraged that he dared to take a scalpel to scripture, or comforted that he was successful in this delicate operation. Yet no matter their interpretation of the book itself, Jefferson would have been gratified to know that, two hundred years later, all are free to debate the meaning of his work, choosing for themselves what to believe.

Bible as Barrow

This book began with talk of excavation, both Jefferson's youthful zeal for exploring burial mounds in the Virginia hills and his mature passion for digging into miraculous scripture in search of its rational bones. Given the meticulous attention paid to all things Jeffersonian, it was perhaps inevitable that the product of the latter would one day become a virtual archaeological site all its own.

In preparation for a 2011 exhibition of *The Life and Morals of Jesus of Nazareth* at the Smithsonian Institution's National Museum of American History (where I have been the Curator of American Religious History since 2016), conservators and curators undertook a concerted effort to preserve the book for the future.

One hundred ninety-one years after its creation, Jefferson's Gospel collage had fallen into serious fragility, with pages brittle, discolored, and generally showing their age. Much of this wear and tear had already been evident when the first images made of the book were captured for the 1904 photolithographic facsimile edition published by the U.S. Government Printing Office, whose black and white photographs also helped document the book's previous deterioration when compared to its current state. As the museum's senior paper conservator Janice Stagnitto Ellis wrote in a companion volume to the 2011 exhibition, by 1904 "the pages had already begun to tear at the edges from handling and use. Several page openings . . . were severely darkened, probably from exposure to natural light, gaslight, and their pollutants while the artifact was on display."[1] Through the century that followed, the book had become too delicate to open safely. Jefferson's glue had hardened the paper and caused it to crack, and the binding was so inflexible that the tension it created was now a threat to the pages it held.

Over time, even as the Jefferson Bible became acknowledged as a national treasure and remained an object of enduring fascination, the Smithsonian had limited public access to it, advising that it be shown only with its covers barely open, obscuring Jefferson's careful work within. If *The Life and Morals* was to be returned fully to view, the museum's experts determined, it would need to be taken apart and pieced back together in order to be repaired, stabilized, and protected in perpetuity.

While primarily a rescue operation, the 2011 conservation effort also offered the opportunity to learn more about the Jefferson Bible than had ever been known before— indeed, more than ever could have been known before the development of a variety of twenty-first-century technologies. Museum conservators discovered that the book was made of twelve types of paper, ten varieties of ink (six in the printed matter and four in handwritten notes), two adhesives, threading of both linen and silk, and goatskin leather. To track the damage suffered by these various materials, the conservation team developed a custom-made database populated through answering approximately two hundred questions per manuscript page, collecting data points numbering in the tens of thousands. They took samples measured in microns for analysis by the Smithsonian's Museum Conservation Institute, which determined the chemical composition of the various inks, and discovered that Jefferson had used both animal collagen and starch paste to reassemble his shorn Bible verses.

Constructed with little more than a penknife and glue, the book yielded new secrets thanks to micro-X-ray fluorescence, infrared spectroscopy, and high-resolution digital imagery. Yet some of the most intriguing insights offered by the Jefferson Bible's conservation came simply from giving the book the kind of careful scrutiny it had not previously received. Though its content and the motives of its maker had been debated for more than a century, few had taken the trouble to take a closer look at the object itself.

Had any done so, it might have been noted long before now that, within the pages of *The Life and Morals of Jesus of Nazareth* and two extant English New Testaments used to fashion it, Jefferson left intriguing remnants of his editorial process, glimpses of the labor and deliberations required to sculpt in the medium of holy writ.

Tucked in among the source books' pages were snippets Jefferson removed but did not glue in place with the others. Collectively, those pieces are Jefferson's cutting room floor: verses seemingly selected but then rejected upon reflection, others perhaps removed in error. In either case, they all provide a view of his accomplishment that is easy to miss when only the finished work is considered. The Jefferson Bible was built with individual folios of paper, each no more than a few inches tall and wide. To see the isolated fragments they all once were is to appreciate the twofold nature of the puzzle maker's art: first in the separation of the original image into slivers of itself, and then in their surprising recombination.

For the most part, these textual leftovers offer little new insight on their own. Many of the two dozen or so scraps (most of which are double sided, with portions of Gospel text on each side) contain nothing miraculous or otherwise out of step with the intentions laid out in Jefferson's correspondence. They could have fit quite naturally into a reason-tested account of Jesus's life. To take one unattached fragment for example, the decision to select, clip, but then not make use of Matthew 27:1–2 may have been merely one of narrative pacing.

> When the morning was come, all the chief priests and elders of the people took counsel against Jesus to put him to death: And when they had bound him, they led him away, and delivered him to Pontius Pilate the governor.

The verses Jefferson ultimately employed to show Jesus condemned (Mark 14: 63–65) and delivered to Pilate (John 18: 28–31) are both more dramatic and concise than Matthew's account here. Still it is worth noting that, in this instance and likely others, Jefferson seems to have weighed one telling against another, even to the point of choosing multiple versions of the same events to compare side-by-side before making a final decision.

Other unused clippings are more intriguing. A few even offer an invitation for new interpretations of Jefferson's motives. A fragment showing Mark 4:26–28 on one side and

Mark 4:39–40 on the other poses the question as to whether Jefferson clipped it to include the opening verses of the mustard seed parable in the former, or a passage in which Jesus commands the wind to stop blowing in the latter. Knowing Jefferson's preference for teachings over miracles, the answer seems plain—until one recalls that Mark 4:26–28 already appears in *The Life and Morals*, raising the possibility that, at least for a moment, Jefferson considered including a scene in which storm winds shook a boat carrying Jesus and his disciples until they cried out in fear. "Master carest not that we perish?" the Apostles wail in this unglued clipping, to which Jesus reacts with divine pique.

And he arose, and rebuked the wind, and said unto the sea, Peace, be still. And the wind ceased, and there was a great calm. And he said unto them, Why are ye so fearful? how is it that ye have no faith?

Of course, including such a passage would be entirely out of keeping with Jefferson's project. His supremely reasonable Jesus elsewhere claims no such sway over the weather. But might these unused verses tell another tale about sympathies lurking behind the selected texts? The disconnected fragments offer several such alluring, if farfetched, possibilities.

Blocks of text were not all that was found when the Jefferson Bible was deconstructed. During its process of assessment and repair of the book, the Smithsonian conservation team found three hairs among the pages, one partially glued beneath the extracted verses. Subsequent testing has been conducted to determine whether any of these hairs may have belonged to Jefferson himself. Given that he worked for hours with a sharp implement and strong adhesive, it is not only possible but probable that small hairs from his fingers or arms, or stray locks drooping from his head as he bowed to set a verse in place, might have become affixed to the sheaf of paper either before it was sent to the bindery, or perhaps after, as he made the book his nightly reading.

At the time of this writing, research on the hairs exhumed from the two-hundred-year-old volume is ongoing. Together with data gleaned from other samples of Jefferson family DNA, they may yet provide further information related to parts of his legacy that extend well beyond his interest in religion, including possible evidence for his likely paternity of Sally Hemings' children. That a book Jefferson hoped to keep hidden might provide clues to births he hoped to keep secret would be the kind of posthumous poetic justice only science can bring.

Whatever may come of this avenue of analysis, the mere fact that there are physical traces embedded within the cut-and-paste pages makes one thing clear. Conceived as a corrective to irrational religiosity and embarrassing superstitions, the Jefferson Bible has somehow become the perfect reliquary. The book turns out to be a repository not just of Jefferson's beliefs—that religion and reason could be reconciled, that even for a heretic and a revolutionary, the stubborn influence of tradition perdures—but also of his body. In a literal sense, *The Life and Morals of Jesus of Nazareth* holds what remains of its creator. Since its rediscovery, every generation of Americans has turned to it to learn what they might about the man who made it, using every new tool at hand. With Jefferson himself as guide, we continue to dig.

ILLUSTRATIONS

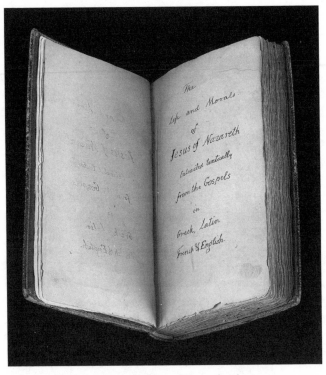

FIGURE I. *The Life and Morals of Jesus of Nazareth*, title page

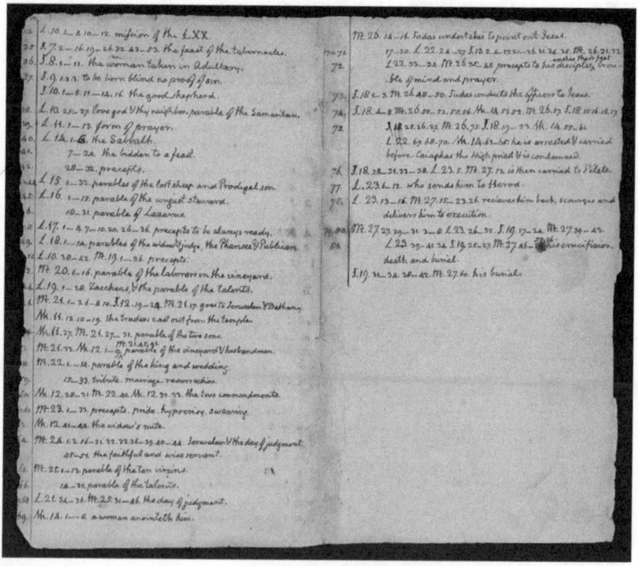

L. 10. 1–8. 10–12. mission of the LXX.
J. 7. 2–16. 19–26. 32. 43–53. the feast of the tabernacles.
J. 8. 1–11. the woman taken in Adultery.
J. 9. 1. 2. 3. to be born blind no proof of sin.
J. 10. 1–5. 11–14. 16. the good shepherd.
L. 10. 25–37. love god & thy neighbor. parable of the Samaritan.
L. 11. 1–13. form of prayer.
L. 14. 1–6. the Sabbath.
7–24. the bidden to a feast.
28–32. precepts.
L. 15. 1–32. parables of the lost sheep and Prodigal son.
L. 16. 1–15. parable of the unjust steward.
19–31. parable of Lazarus.
L. 17. 1–4. 7–10. 20. 26–36. precepts to be always ready.
L. 18. 1–14. parables of the widow & judge, the Pharisee & Publican.
L. 10. 38–42. Mt. 19. 1–26. precepts.
Mt. 20. 1–16. parable of the labourers in the vineyard.
L. 19. 1–28. Zaccheus, & the parable of the talents.
Mt. 21. 1–3. 6–8. 10. J. 12. 19–24. Mt. 21. 17. goes to Jerusalem & Bethany.
Mk. 11. 12. 15–19. the traders cast out from the temple.
Mk. 11. 27. Mt. 21. 27–32. parable of the two sons.
Mt. 21. 33. Mk. 12. 1–9. Mt. 21. 45. 46. parable of the vineyard & husbandmen.
Mt. 22. 1–14. parable of the king and wedding.
15–33. tribute. marriage. resurrection.
Mk. 12. 28–31. Mt. 22. 40. Mk. 12. 32. 33. the two commandments.
Mt. 23. 1–33. precepts. pride. hypocrisy. swearing.
Mk. 12. 41–44. the widow's mite.
Mt. 24. 1. 2. 16–21. 32. 33. 36–39. 40–44. Jerusalem & the day of judgment.
45–51. the faithful and wise servant.
Mt. 25. 1–13. parable of the ten virgins.
14–30. parable of the talents.
L. 21. 34–36. Mt. 25. 31–46. the day of judgment.
Mk. 14. 1–8. a woman anointeth him.

Mt. 26. 14–16. Judas undertakes to point out Jesus.
17–20. L. 22. 24–27. J. 13. 2. 4–17. 21–26. 31. 34. 35. Mt. 26. 31. 33.
72. L. 22. 33–34. Mt. 26. 35–45. precepts to his disciples, washes their feet, trouble of mind and prayer.
73. J. 18. 1–3. Mt. 26. 48–50. Judas conducts the officers to Jesus.
74. J. 18. 4–8. Mt. 26. 50–52. 55. 56. Mk. 14. 51. 52. Mt. 26. 57. J. 18. 15. 16. 18. 17.
75. J. 18. 25. 26. 27. Mt. 26. 75. J. 18. 19–23. Mk. 14. 55–61.
L. 22. 67. 68. 70. Mk. 14. 63–65. he is arrested & carried before Caiaphas the High priest & is condemned.
76. J. 18. 28–31. 33–38. L. 23. 5. Mt. 27. 13. is then carried to Pilate.
77. L. 23. 6–12. who sends him to Herod.
78. L. 23. 13–16. Mt. 27. 15–23. 26. receives him back, scourges and delivers him to execution.
Mt. 27. 27. 29–31. 3–8. L. 23. 26–32. J. 19. 17–24. Mt. 27. 39–43.
L. 23. 39–41. 34. J. 19. 25–27. Mt. 27. 46–50. his crucifixion, death and burial.
J. 19. 31–34. 38–42. Mt. 27. 60. his burial.

FIGURE 2. *The Life and Morals of Jesus of Nazareth*, index

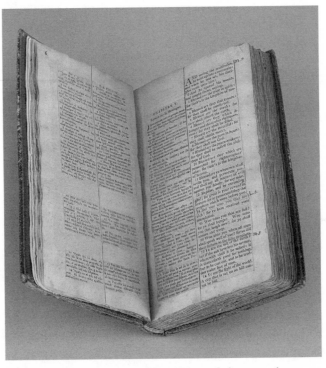

FIGURE 3. *The Life and Morals of Jesus of Nazareth*, four text columns

FIGURE 4. New Testament source book

FIGURE 5. Cyrus Adler

FIGURE 6. John Fletcher Lacey

INTRODUCTION: EXCAVATING THE SACRED

1. Quotations from the discussion of Jefferson's investigation of the barrows are from Thomas Jefferson, *Notes on the State of Virginia* (Boston: Lilly and Wait, 1832), 100–104.

2. See for example, Ronald Hatzenbuehler, "Questioning Whether Thomas Jefferson Was the 'Father' of American Archaeology," *History and Anthropology*, Volume 22, 121–29.

3. "From Thomas Jefferson to William Short, 31 October 1819," *Founders Online,* National Archives, accessed September 6, 2019, https://founders.archives.gov/documents/Jefferson/98-01-02-0850.

4. "Thomas Jefferson to John Adams, 24 January 1814," *Founders Online,* National Archives, accessed April 11, 2019, https://founders.archives.gov/documents/Jefferson/03-07-02-0083. [Original source: *The Papers of Thomas Jefferson*, Retirement Series, vol. 7, *28 November 1813 to 30 September 1814*, ed. J. Jefferson Looney. Princeton: Princeton University Press, 2010, pp. 146–151.]

5. "Thomas Jefferson to Francis Adrian Van der Kemp, 30 July 1816," *Founders Online,* National Archives, accessed April 11, 2019, https://founders.archives.gov/documents/Jefferson/03-10-02-0167. [Original source: *The Papers of Thomas Jefferson*, Retirement Series, vol. 10, *May 1816 to 18 January 1817*, ed. J. Jefferson Looney. Princeton: Princeton University Press, 2013, pp. 277–278.]

6. "From Thomas Jefferson to William Stephens Smith, 13 November 1787," *Founders Online,* National Archives, accessed April 11, 2019, https://founders.archives.gov/documents/Jefferson/01-12-02-0348. [Original source: *The Papers of Thomas Jefferson*,

vol. 12, *7 August 1787–31 March 1788*, ed. Julian P. Boyd. Princeton: Princeton University Press, 1955, pp. 355–357.]

7. Thomas Jefferson, *The Life and Morals of Jesus of Nazareth. Extracted textually from the Gospels in Greek, Latin, French, and English* (Washington, DC: Government Printing Office, 1904).

8. Thomas Jefferson, *The life and morals of Jesus of Nazareth: extracted textually from the Gospels, together with a comparison of His doctrines with those of others* (St. Louis: N. D. Thompson, 1902).

9. Thomas Jefferson, *The Jefferson Bible*, ed. Douglas Lurton (New York: Grosset & Dunlap, 1940), v.

10. Adams, Dickinson W, ed. *Jefferson's Extracts from the Gospels. The Philosophy of Jesus and The Life and Morals of Jesus.* (Princeton: Princeton University Press, 1983).

11. For Unitarian influenced editions see *The Jefferson Bible*, with an introduction by Douglas Harrington (New York: C.N. Potter, 1964), and *The Jefferson Bible: The Life and Morals of Jesus of Nazareth*, with an introduction by Forest Church (Boston: Beacon Press, 2001).

12. *The Jefferson Bible, Smithsonian Edition: The Life and Morals of Jesus of Nazareth* (Washington, DC: Smithsonian Books, 2011).

CHAPTER 1. SHARPENING THE BLADE

1. Quotes from *De heretico comburendo* are from James Thomas Law, *The ecclesiastical statutes at large, extr. and arranged by J. T. Law*, Volume 3, (London: William Benning and Co, 1847), 176. For Jefferson's commentary on these laws, see Thomas Jefferson, *Notes on the State of Virginia* (Boston: Lilly and Wait, 1832), 165.

2. Jefferson, 1832, 165.

3. Edwin Gaustad, *Sworn on the Altar of God: A Religious Biography of Thomas Jefferson* (Grand Rapids: Wm. B. Eerdmans Publishing, 1996), 8–15.

4. Henry Stephens Randall, *The life of Thomas Jefferson* (New York: Derby Jackson, 1858), Volume 1, 17.

5. Ibid., 18.

6. "From Thomas Jefferson to J. P. P. Derieux, 25 July 1788," *Founders Online,* National Archives, accessed April 11, 2019, https://founders.archives.gov/documents/Jefferson/01-13-02 -0302. [Original source: *The Papers of Thomas Jefferson*, vol. 13, *March–7 October 1788*, ed. Julian P. Boyd. Princeton: Princeton University Press, 1956, pp. 418–419.]

7. Gaustad, 11.

8. Thomas Jefferson, *Memoir, correspondence, and miscellanies from the papers of Thomas Jefferson*, Volumes 1–2, (Boston: Gray and Bowen, 1830), 2.

9. "From Thomas Jefferson to John Trumbull, 15 February 1789," *Founders Online*, National Archives, accessed April 11, 2019, https://founders.archives.gov/documents/Jefferson/01-14-02 -0321. [Original source: *The Papers of Thomas Jefferson*, vol. 14, *8 October 1788–26 March 1789*, ed. Julian P. Boyd. Princeton: Princeton University Press, 1958, p. 561.]

10. Gaustad, 21.

11. James Boswell, *Life of Johnson: Volume 1*, (London: J. Davis, 1830), 312.

12. "From Thomas Jefferson to John Garland Jefferson, 11 June 1790," *Founders Online,* National Archives, accessed April 11, 2019, https://founders.archives.gov/documents/Jefferson/01-16-02 -0278. [Original source: *The Papers of Thomas Jefferson*, vol. 16, *30 November 1789–4 July 1790*, ed. Julian P. Boyd. Princeton: Princeton University Press, 1961, pp. 480–482.]

13. Henry St. John Bolingbroke, *The works of Lord Bolingbroke: with a life, prepared expressly for this edition, containing additional information relative to his personal and public character* (Philadelphia: Carey and Hart, 1841), 32.

14. Ibid., 389.

15. Ibid. For its quotation by Jefferson see *The Literary Bible of Thomas Jefferson: His Commonplace Book of Philosophers and Poets* (New York: Greenwood Press, 1928), 49.

16. Bolingbroke, 389.

17. Ibid., 406. For its quotation by Jefferson see *The Literary Bible of Thomas Jefferson*, 50.

18. Bolingbroke, 406.

19. Quoted by Jefferson in *The Literary Bible of Thomas Jefferson: His Commonplace Book of Philosophers and Poets* (New York: Greenwood Press, 1928), 56.

20. Henry St. John Bolingbroke, *The Works of Henry St. John, Lord Viscount Bolingbroke in Five Volumes Complete* (1754), Volume 4, 283. For its quotation by Jefferson see *The Literary Bible of Thomas Jefferson*, 57.

21. Bolingbroke, 1841, 304. For its quotation by Jefferson see *The Literary Bible of Thomas Jefferson*, 57.

22. Ibid., 491.

23. Jefferson, 1832, 166.

24. This and subsequent quotations, "From Thomas Jefferson to Peter Carr, with Enclosure, 10 August 1787," *Founders Online,* National Archives, accessed April 11, 2019, https://founders.archives.gov/documents/Jefferson/01-12-02-0021. [Original source: *The Papers of Thomas Jefferson*, vol. 12, *7 August 1787–31 March 1788*, ed. Julian P. Boyd. Princeton: Princeton University Press, 1955, pp. 14–19.]

CHAPTER 2. MAKING THE CUT

1. "Galileo Galilei to Belisario Vinto," 1610, quoted in Mary Allan-Olney, *The Private Life of Galileo* (London: Macmillan and Co., 1870), 41.

2. John Bernard, *Retrospections of America, 1797–1811* (New York: Harper and Brothers, 1887), 238.

3. Joseph Priestley, *A History of the Corruptions of Christianity* (London: The British and Foreign Unitarian Aid Association, 1871), 2.

4. Ibid.

5. Ibid., 1.

6. Ibid., 2.

7. John Towill Rutt, *Life and correspondence of Joseph Priestley,* Volume 2 (London: Hunter, 1832), 372.

8. Ibid., 373.

9. Timothy Dwight, *The Duty of Americans at this Present Crisis* (New Haven: Thomas and Samuel Green, 1798), 20.

10. Rutt, 372.

11. This and quotations following, "From Thomas Jefferson to Joseph Priestley, 9 April 1803," *Founders Online*, National Archives, accessed April 11, 2019, https://founders.archives.gov /documents/Jefferson/01-40-02-0124. [Original source: *The Papers of Thomas Jefferson*, vol. 40, *4 March–10 July 1803*, ed. Barbara B. Oberg. Princeton: Princeton University Press, 2013, pp. 157–159.]

12. Here and quotations following, "From Thomas Jefferson to Benjamin Rush, 21 April 1803," *Founders Online,* National Archives, accessed April 11, 2019, https://founders.archives.gov /documents/Jefferson/01-40-02-0178-0001. [Original source: *The Papers of Thomas Jefferson*, vol. 40, *4 March–10 July 1803*, ed. Barbara B. Oberg. Princeton: Princeton University Press, 2013, pp. 251–253.]

13. Here and quotations following, "Thomas Jefferson to John Adams, 12 October 1813," *Founders Online,* National Archives, accessed April 11, 2019, https://founders.archives.gov/documents /Jefferson/03-06-02-0431. [Original source: *The Papers of Thomas Jefferson*, Retirement Series, vol. 6, *11 March to 27 November 1813*, ed. J. Jefferson Looney. Princeton: Princeton University Press, 2009, pp. 548–552.]

14. Dickinson Adams, ed., *Jefferson's Extracts from the Gospels: The Philosophy of Jesus and The Life and Morals of Jesus* (Princeton: Princeton University Press, 2014), 28.

15. *Federal Republican* (Washington, DC), October 11, 1814.

16. *Portland Gazette,* November 7, 1814.

17. *Federal Republican*, January 31, 1815.

18. *Virginia Patriot* (Richman, Virginia), February 8, 1815.

19. For the full debate see Annals of Congress, House of Representatives, 13th Congress, 3rd Session, 1105-6 (1814–15).

20. See Frank Lambert, "'God—and a Religious President . . . [or] Jefferson and No God': Campaigning for a Voter-Imposed Religious Test in 1800," *Journal of Church and State*, Vol. 39, No. 4 (Autumn 1997), pp. 769–789.

21. Editorial, *Connecticut Courant* (Hartford, Connecticut), September 15, 1800.

22. "Testimonial for Charles Clay, [15 August 1779]," *Founders Online,* National Archives, accessed April 11, 2019, https://founders.archives.gov/documents/Jefferson/01-03-02-0076. [Original source: *The Papers of Thomas Jefferson*, vol. 3, *18 June 1779–30 September 1780*, ed. Julian P. Boyd. Princeton: Princeton University Press, 1951, p. 67.]

23. All quotations of Charles Clay can be found in "Charles Clay to Thomas Jefferson, 20 December 1814," *Founders Online,* National Archives, accessed April 11, 2019, https://founders.archives.gov/documents/Jefferson/03-08-02-0130. [Original source: *The Papers of Thomas Jefferson*, Retirement Series, vol. 8, *1 October 1814 to 31 August 1815*, ed. J. Jefferson Looney. Princeton: Princeton University Press, 2011, pp. 149–150.]

24. "Thomas Jefferson to Charles Clay, 29 January 1815, *Founders Online,* National Archives, accessed April 11, 2019, https://founders.archives.gov/documents/Jefferson/03-08-02-0181. [Original source: *The Papers of Thomas Jefferson*, Retirement Series, vol. 8, *1 October 1814 to 31 August 1815*, ed. J. Jefferson Looney. Princeton: Princeton University Press, 2011, pp. 211–213.]

25. "Thomas Jefferson to Charles Thomson, 9 January 1816," *Founders Online,* National Archives, accessed April 11, 2019, https://founders.archives.gov/documents/Jefferson/03-09-02-0216. [Original source: *The Papers of Thomas Jefferson*, Retirement Series, vol. 9, *September 1815 to April 1816*, ed. J. Jefferson Looney. Princeton: Princeton University Press, 2012, pp. 340–342.]

26. Margaret Bayard Smith in Gaillard Hunt, ed., *The first forty years of Washington society, portrayed by the family letters of Mrs. Samuel Harrison Smith (Margaret Bayard) from the collection of her grandson, J. Henley Smith* (New York: Scribner, 1906), 385.

27. "From Thomas Jefferson to James Madison, 7 May 1783," *Founders Online,* National Archives, accessed April 11, 2019, https://founders.archives.gov/documents/Jefferson/01-06-02 -0246. [Original source: *The Papers of Thomas Jefferson*, vol. 6, *21 May 1781–1 March 1784*, ed. Julian P. Boyd. Princeton: Princeton University Press, 1952, pp. 265–267.]

28. "To Thomas Jefferson from William Short, 1 December 1819," *Founders Online,* National Archives, accessed August 11, 2019, https://founders.archives.gov/documents/Jefferson/98-01 -02-0928. [This is an Early Access document from The Papers of Thomas Jefferson: Retirement Series. It is not an authoritative final version.]

29. Here and quotations following, "From Thomas Jefferson to William Short, 13 April 1820," *Founders Online,* National Archives, accessed April 11, 2019, https://founders.archives.gov /documents/Jefferson/98-01-02-1218. [This is an Early Access document from The Papers of Thomas Jefferson: Retirement Series. It is not an authoritative final version.]

30. This and subsequent quotations from Jefferson's August 1820 letter on *The Life and Morals*, "From Thomas Jefferson to William Short, 4 August 1820," *Founders Online,* National Archives, accessed April 11, 2019, https://founders.archives.gov/documents /Jefferson/98-01-02-1438.

CHAPTER 3: THE QUEST FOR
THE JEFFERSONIAN JESUS

1. Robert W. Funk, Roy W. Hoover, and the Jesus Seminar, *The Five Gospels: The Search for the Authentic Words of Jesus: New Translation and Commentary* (New York: Macmillan, 1993), v.

2. Robert W. Funk et al., "Jesus Seminar Phase 1: Sayings of Jesus: Example from Luke 6:29–37," Westar Institute, accessed July 12, 2019, https://www.westarinstitute.org/projects/the-jesus -seminar/jesus-seminar-phase-1-sayings-of-jesus/example-from -luke-629-37/.

3. Robert W. Funk, "The Jesus Seminar: Opening Remarks," Westar Institute, accessed July 12, 2019, https://www.westarinstitute.org/projects/jesus-seminar-opening-remarks/.

4. Ibid.

5. Richard B. Hays, "The Corrected Jesus," *First Things*, May 1994. https://www.firstthings.com/article/1994/05/the-corrected-jesus.

6. "The Jesus Seminar: Voting," Westar Institute, https://www.westarinstitute.org/projects/the-jesus-seminar/voting/.

7. Reimarus, quoted in Albert Schweitzer, *The Quest of the Historical Jesus: A Critical Study of Its Progress from Reimarus to Wrede* (London: Adam and Charles Black: 1910), 16.

8. Ibid., 22.

9. Ibid., 16.

10. Ibid., 17.

11. Ibid., 20.

12. Robert W. Funk, "Milestones in the Quest for the Historical Jesus," *The Fourth R*, Volume 14-4, July–August 2001.

13. Schweitzer, 15.

14. Funk, 2001.

15. Schweitzer, 29.

16. Ibid.

17. David Friedrich Strauss, *The Life of Jesus Critically Examined* (London: Sonnenschein, 1892), 39.

18. Except where otherwise noted, in my reading of *The Life and Morals of Jesus of Nazareth* I have relied on the most recent facsimile, *The Jefferson Bible: The Smithsonian Edition* (Washington, DC: Smithsonian Books, 2011). Jefferson's pagination made use of a single page number for each verso and recto, with the Greek and Latin text columns on the former, and the French and English on the latter. For the book's opening with "Κεφ β, Caput II, Chap II," see *The Life and Morals of Jesus of Nazareth*, 1.

19. "From Thomas Jefferson to William Short, 31 October 1819," *Founders Online,* National Archives, accessed April 11, 2019, https://founders.archives.gov/documents/Jefferson/98-01-02-0850.

20. *The Life and Morals of Jesus of Nazareth*, 1.

21. "From Thomas Jefferson to William Short, 4 August 1820," *Founders Online*, National Archives, accessed September 29, 2019, https://founders.archives.gov/documents/Jefferson/98-01 -02-1438. [This is an Early Access document from The Papers of Thomas Jefferson: Retirement Series. It is not an authoritative final version.]

22. *The Life and Morals of Jesus of Nazareth*, 1.

23. "From Thomas Jefferson to William Short, 13 April 1820," *Founders Online,* National Archives, accessed September 13, 2019, https://founders.archives.gov/documents/Jefferson/98-01 -02-1218.

24. *The Life and Morals of Jesus of Nazareth*, 15.

25. Ibid., 16.

26. Ibid., 2.

27. Ibid., 82.

CHAPTER 4: LOST AND FOUND

1. For details of Cyrus Adler's biography and early years with U.S. National Museum, see his autobiography *I Have Considered the Days* (Philadelphia: Jewish Publication Society of America, 1941).

2. Cyrus Adler and I. M. Casanowicz, *The Collection of Jewish Ceremonial Objects in the United States National Museum* (Washington, DC: Government Printing Office, 1908), 701–702.

3. For more on the collecting notes of Cyrus Adler and his colleague I. M. Cazanowicz, see my article "Religion and Music at the Smithsonian," *Smithsonian Year of Music* (Blog), March 2017. https://music.si.edu/story/religion-and-music-smithsonian.

4. Adler and Casanowicz, 701-702.

5. Richard Rathbun, *Report on the Progress and Condition of the United States National Museum for the Year Ending June 30, 1914*, special report (Washington, DC: Government Printing Office, 1915), 70.

6. "An Act to Establish the Smithsonian Institution, 1846," facsimile available at https://siarchives.si.edu/history/featured-topics/stories/act-establish-smithsonian-institution-1846.

7. *Report on the Progress and Condition of the United States National Museum for 1914* (Washington, DC: Government Printing Office, 1915), 71.

8. *Report of the U. S. National Museum under the Direction of the Smithsonian Institution for the Year Ending June 30, 1893*, special report (Washington, DC: Government Printing Office, 1895), 761.

9. Ibid., 136.

10. Cyrus Adler, ed., *The Life and Morals of Jesus of Nazareth: Extracted Textually from the Gospels in Greek, Latin, French, and English* (Washington, DC: Government Printing Office, 1904), 10.

11. See Edward Eitches, "Maryland's 'Jew Bill,'" *American Jewish Historical Quarterly* Vol. 60, No. 3, The Colonial and Early National Period (March, 1971), 279.

12. *Catalogue of a Hebrew Library: Being the Collection, with a Few Additions of the Late Joshua I. Cohen*, Compiled by Cyrus Adler (Baltimore: Privately Printed, 1887), 6.

13. *Semi-Weekly Standard* (Raleigh, North Carolina), August 31, 1853.

14. *Bulletin of the University of Virginia Library,* Volume 1 Number 7, May 1916, 31.

15. *Richmond Enquirer* (Richmond, Virginia), July 23 1847, 4.

16. *The Richmond Enquirer*, reprinted in *The Evening Post* (New York, New York), August 10, 1847, 1–2.

17. Henry S. Randall, *The Life of Thomas Jefferson*, Volume 3, (Philadelphia: J.B. Lippincott & Co., 1865), 451.

18. Francis D. Cogliano, *Thomas Jefferson: Reputation and Legacy* (Charlottesville: University of Virginia Press, 2008), 78.

19. Adler, 9–10.

20. Cyrus Adler, Immanuel M. Casanowicz, *Biblical Antiquities: A Description of the Exhibit at the Cotton States Exposition* (Washington, DC: Government Printing Office, 1898), 953.

21. Ibid., 1023.

22. *The Atlanta Constitution* (Atlanta, Georgia), August 23, 1895, 9.

23. Ibid.

24. "A Valuable Collection on Exhibition at Atlanta Fair," *Democrat and Chronicle*, (Rochester, New York), September 29, 1895, 7.

25. Cyrus Adler, "The American Religious Scene," in *Lectures, Selected Papers, Addresses*. (Privately published, 1933), 356.

CHAPTER 5: BORN AGAIN

1. "Jefferson Bible to be Issued," *Des Moines Register* (Des Moines, Iowa), July 11, 1904, 3.

2. Ibid.

3. Ibid.

4. See for example "The Jefferson Bible Found in Washington," *San Francisco Chronicle*, July 29, 1900, 26.

5. *Des Moines Register* (Des Moines, Iowa), July 11, 1904, 3.

6. *San Francisco Chronicle,* July 29, 1900, 26.

7. John F. Lacey, *Major John F. Lacey, Memorial Volume* (Cedar Rapids: Iowa Park and Forestry Association, 1919), 385.

8. Ibid., 389.

9. T. Adolphus Trollope, "Some Recollections of Hiram Powers," *Lippincott's Magazine of Popular Literature and Science*, February 1, 1875, 208.

10. Ibid., 316.

11. Lacey's report on his encounter with *The Life and Morals of Jesus of Nazareth* was widely reprinted and read into the Congressional Record, from which this text is taken. Congressional Record: Proceedings and Debates of the Fifty-seventh Congress, First Session (Washington, DC: Government Printing Office, 1902), 5272.

12. Ibid.

13. Quotations from the debate prompted by Rep. Lacey also appear in the Congressional Record, as in note 11.

14. "The Jefferson Bible," *The Inter Ocean* (Chicago, Illinois), Jun 18, 1902, 6.

15. *The Catholic Advance* (Wichita, Kansas), May 29, 1902, 1.

16. "Tupper Condemns Jefferson's Bible," *The Times* (Philadelphia, Pennsylvania), 19 May 1902, 5.

17. Here and quotations following, "Ministers Oppose Jefferson's Bible," *The Times* (Philadelphia, Pennsylvania), June 3, 1902, 7.

18. "The Bible of Thomas Jefferson," *Jewish Comment* 20, no. 21 (March 3, 1905), 2. Quoted in Greg Robinson, "Resurrection and Life: Cyrus Adler and the Jefferson Bible," *American Jewish Archives Journal*, Vol. 63, No. 1 (2011), 11.

19. "Jefferson's 'Bible,'" *Richmond Dispatch*, May 27, 1902, 5.

20. Quotation from the *Washington Post* reprinted as "Thomas Jefferson's Bible," in the *Richmond Dispatch*, May 22, 1902, 4.

21. Ibid.

22. "Congressmen Think Again," *The Oskaloosa Times* (Oskaloosa, Kansas), June 20, 1902, 2.

23. "The Jefferson Bible," *The Inter Ocean* (Chicago, Illinois), June 18, 1902, 6.

24. "A Metcalfe Thompson," *The Courier-Journal* (Louisville, Kentucky), October 28, 1899, 6.

25. "The Jefferson Bible," *St. Louis Globe-Democrat*, June 21, 1902, 6.

26. *The Life and Morals of Jesus of Nazareth*, 5.

27. Thomas Jefferson, *The Life and Morals of Jesus of Nazareth*, ed. N. D. Thompson (St. Louis: N. D. Thompson, 1902), 29.

28. Cyrus Adler, *I Have Considered the Days* (Philadelphia: Jewish Publication Society of America, 1941), 58.

CHAPTER 6: SOCIAL ENGINEERING

1. *The Survey*, Volume 50, January 1, 1923, 543.

2. *The Gazette* (Cedar Rapids, Iowa), December 4, 1922, 13.

3. Ibid.

4. Henry Jackson, *Robinson Crusoe, social engineer; how the discovery of Robinson Crusoe solves the labor problem and opens the path to industrial peace* (New York: E.P Button & Company, 1922), 3.

5. Henry E. Jackson, ed., *The Thomas Jefferson Bible* (New York: Boni and Liveright, 1921), front matter.

6. Ibid., 11.

7. Ibid., 14.

8. *Report on the Progress and Condition of the U.S. National Museum for the Year Ending June 30, 1920*, special report (Washington, DC: Government Printing Office, 1920), 61.

9. Jackson 1921, 134.

10. Ibid., 15.

11. Ibid., 16.

12. Ibid., 18.

13. Ibid., 30.

14. Ibid., 33.

15. Ibid., 57–58.

16. Ibid., 99.

17. Ibid., 100.

18. Ibid., 89–90.

19. Ibid., 74–75.

20. Thomas L. Masson, *The World's Work: A History of Our Time*, Volume 47 (New York: Doubleday, Doran, 1923), 233.

21. Ibid.

22. Herbert Quick, "The Bible and Thomas Jefferson," *Knoxville News Sentinel*, February 14, 1924, 4.

23. "Statement of Henry E. Jackson, President Social Engineering Institute," Hearings in the Committee on Finance of the United States Senate (Washington, DC: Government Printing Office, 1935), 1109.

CHAPTER 7: CONGRESSIONAL INHERITANCES

1. Franklin Delano Roosevelt, "Address at the Laying of the Cornerstone of the Jefferson Memorial, Washington, DC," November 15, 1939, American Presidency Project,

https://www.presidency.ucsb.edu/documents/address-the
-cornerstone-laying-the-jefferson-memorial-washington-dc.

2. *The Courier-Journal* (Louisville, Kentucky), December 11, 1904, 17.

3. *Variety*, May 1939.

4. Here and quotes following from the introduction to *The Jefferson Bible, Selected by Thomas Jefferson*, edited with foreword by Douglas Lurton, (New York: Wilfred Funk, 1940), v.

5. Douglas Lurton, *My Mother's Bible: A Scrapbook Treasury of Verse and Wisdom* (New York: Wilfred Funk, 1941).

6. "News to Publish 'The Jefferson Bible' in Serial Form," *Birmingham News* (Birmingham, Alabama), December 15, 1940, 84.

7. "Trends of the Times," *Dayton Daily News*, December 18, 1944, 10.

8. Thomas Jefferson, *The Jefferson Bible*, ed. Forest Church (Boston: Beacon Press, 1989), vii.

9. Ibid.

10. Dan Cryer, *Being Alive and Having to Die: The Spiritual Odyssey of Forest Church* (New York: Saint Martin's Press, 2011), 48.

11. Ibid.

12. Ibid.

13. Ibid., 93.

14. "Rev. Forrest Church, Who Embraced a Gospel of Service, Dies at 61," *New York Times*, September 25, 2009.

15. Jefferson, *The Jefferson Bible* (1989), vii.

16. Ibid.

17. "From Thomas Jefferson to Benjamin Waterhouse, 26 June 1822," *Founders Online*, National Archives, accessed August 11, 2019, https://founders.archives.gov/documents/Jefferson/98-01-02-2905.

CHAPTER 8: JEFFERSON, JESUS, AND THE SIXTIES

1. *Glens Falls Times* (Glens Falls, New York), December 15, 1968, 22.

2. Sam Roberts, "Donald S. Harrington, 91, Liberal Crusader," *New York Times*, September 20, 2005, 26.

3. *Daily Independent Journal* (San Rafael, California), June 13, 1959, 28.

4. Thomas Jefferson, *The Jefferson Bible, With the Annotated Commentaries on Religion of Thomas Jefferson*, Introduction by Henry Wilder Foote; Foreword by Donald S. Harrington; Edited by O. I. A. Roche (New York: Clarkson N. Potter, Inc., 1964). Quotations from Harrington throughout are from his foreword to the edition.

5. Harrington, 13.

6. *Des Moines Tribune*, November 8, 1962,14.

7. Ibid.

8. Ibid.

9. Ibid.

10. Thomas Jefferson, *The Jefferson Bible, being the life & morals of Jesus Christ of Nazareth extracted textually from the Gospels of Matthew, Mark, Luke & John by Thomas Jefferson* (Greenwich, Connecticut: Fawcett, 1961).

11. *The Morning Call* (Allentown, Pennsylvania), December 19, 1963, 18.

12. *Beckley Post-Herald* (West Virginia) July 2, 1963, 4.

13. Leo L. Rockwell, letter to the editor, *Tampa Tribune* December 23, 1963.

14. "From Thomas Jefferson to Thomas B. Parker, 15 May 1819," *Founders Online,* National Archives, accessed July 9, 2019, https://founders.archives.gov/documents/Jefferson/98-01-02 -0407. [This is an Early Access document from The Papers of Thomas Jefferson: Retirement Series. It is not an authoritative final version.]

15. Harrington, 9.

16. Ibid., 11.

17. Ibid.

18. Ibid., 11-12.

19. Ibid., 12.

20. Ibid., 13.

21. Ibid.

22. Thomas Jefferson, *Thomas Jefferson's Human Jesus* (New York: Eakins Press, 1968).

23. Adam Clatyon Powell, Jr., *Times-Advocate* (Escondido, California), May 17, 1963, 3.

24. Adam Clayton Powell, Jr., *Adam by Adam: The Autobiography of Adam Clayton Powell, Jr* (New York: Kensington, 1971), 43–44.

CHAPTER 9: CHOOSE YOUR OWN ADVENTURE

1. WallBuilders web site: https://wallbuilders.com/about-us/.

2. Erik Eckholm, "Using History to Mold Ideas on the Right," *New York Times,* May 4, 2011.

3. David Baron, *America's Godly Heritage* (Aledo, Texas: Wallbuilder Press, 1993).

4. *County of Allegheny v. American Civil Liberties Union*, 492 U.S. 573 (1989).

5. Barton enjoyed a brief brush with mainstream fame through an appearance on the *Daily Show*, May 4, 2001, during which he and the comedian Jon Stewart discussed the letter in question. Available online at http://www.cc.com/video-clips/bk6j07/the-daily-show-with-jon-stewart-exclusive---david-barton-extended-interview-pt--1.

6. "From John Adams to Benjamin Rush, 21 December 1809," *Founders Online,* National Archives, accessed April 11, 2019, https://founders.archives.gov/documents/Adams/99-02-02-5485. [This is an Early Access document from The Adams Papers. It is not an authoritative final version.]

7. As Adams wrote to Rush in the letter above (n.6), "Do you wonder that Voltaire and Paine have made Proselytes?"

8. Molly Driscoll, "The 'Jefferson Lies' is Recalled by Publisher Thomas Nelson," *Christian Science Monitor,* August 13, 2012.

9. David Barton, *The Jefferson Lies* (Nashville: Thomas Nelson, 2012), xxiv.

10. Ibid., 68.

11. Ibid., 69.

12. Ibid., 78.

13. "Thomas Jefferson to John Adams, 12 October 1813," *Founders Online,* National Archives, accessed April 11, 2019, https://founders.archives.gov/documents/Jefferson/03-06-02 -0431. [Original source: *The Papers of Thomas Jefferson*, Retirement Series, vol. 6, *11 March to 27 November 1813*, ed. J. Jefferson Looney. Princeton: Princeton University Press, 2009, pp. 548–552.]

14. Jeffrey Trachtenberg, "Publisher Pulls Book on Thomas Jefferson," *Wall Street Journal*, August 10, 2012.

15. Elise Hu, "Publisher Pulls Controversial Jefferson Book," National Public Radio, August 9, 2012.

16. Justin Taylor, "Thomas Nelson Ceases Publication of David Barton's Error-Ridden Book on Jefferson's Faith," *The Gospel Coalition* (blog), August 9, 2012, https://www.thegospelcoalition .org/blogs/justin-taylor/thomas-nelson-ceases-publication-of -david-bartons-error-ridden-book-on-jeffersons-faith/.

17. American Humanist Association, "Scriptures Go Under the Knife in A Jefferson Bible for the Twenty-First Century," press release, January 3, 2013. https://americanhumanist.org/news/2013 -01-scriptures-go-under-the-knife-in-a-jefferson-bible-f/.

18. The Humanist Press's readers' response website, http://jefferson.humanistpress.com, is unfortunately inactive at the time of this writing.

19. Luis Granados, "Introduction," *A Jefferson Bible for the Twenty-First Century* (Washington, DC: Humanist Press, 2012), 7.

20. Ibid.

21. Ibid., 71.

22. Ibid., 72.

23. Ibid., 73.

24. Ibid., 79.

25. Ibid., 86.

26. Ibid., 100.

27. Ibid., 106.

28. Tobias Huch, "Vorwort," *Die Jefferson-Bibel, Der wahre Kern des Neuen Testaments* (Munich: Riva Verlag, 2018), 7.

29. Ibid., 7-8.

EPILOGUE: BIBLE AS BARROW

1. Janice Stagnitto Ellis, "Conservation," in Harry R. Rubenstein, Barbara Clark Smith, and Janice Stagnitto Ellis, *The History and Conservation of the Jefferson Bible* (Washington, DC: Smithsonian Books, 2011), 43.

Adams, Dickinson, 12, 39

Adams, John: election of 1800 between Jefferson and, 43–44; Jefferson's letters to, 6, 38–39, 40, 81, 82, 89, 170; quoted by Barton, 167–68, 171

Adler, Cyrus: anti-Semitic ministers and, 109–10, 118; asking that his name be removed from title page, 116–17; Atlanta exposition in 1895 and, 86–92; creating displays at National Museum, 76–79; discovering Jefferson's mutilated New Testaments, 80–84; discovering original *Life and Morals*, 84–86; as influential public historian, 75; introduction to 1904 edition written by, 11, 102, 106, 109–10, 116–17; Lacey's encounter with, 98; not originally interested in publication, 99; as observant Jew, 75, 91, 106, 109–10; photo of, figure 5 at 190; positions at Smithsonian Institution, 75–76

"The Aims of Jesus and His Disciples" (Reimarus), 58

American Humanist Association, edition published by, 172–76

America's Godly Heritage (Barton), 166, 167

Anglicanism: of Jefferson, 15, 16–17; Jefferson's advocacy against establishment of, 34; of Jefferson's teachers, 18–19; Jefferson's youthful reaction against, 24–25, 32–33

anti-Semitism, of Christian clergymen attacking Adler, 109–10, 118

archaeological excavation, 1–5, 6–7, 179

Armas, Emilio de, 176–77

atheism: Jefferson suspected of, 34, 41, 42, 43–44, 45, 127. *See also* heresy

Atlanta exposition in 1895, 86–92

Babbitt, Clinton, 138

Bachman, Michele, 166

Bacon, Francis, 19

barrows, excavation of, 1–5, 6–7, 179
Barton, David, 166–71, 175
Beacon Press, 12, 142
Beinhard, Franz Volkmax, 60
Belsham, Thomas, 34
Bhagavad Gita, passages in Humanist Press edition, 172
Bible: Adler's exhibit at 1895 Atlanta exposition, 86–92; boom of 1960s in publishing of, 149–50; famous misprints of, 115; Powell on contradictions in, 163; read in public schools, 151–54; as word of God, 6, 16, 163 *See also* Hebrew Bible; New Testament
blasphemy: Jefferson's exposure to Bolingbroke and, 22–23; Jesus Seminar and, 56; sermons attacking Jefferson for, 160. *See also* atheism; heresy
Bok, Edward, 119
Bolingbroke (Henry St. John), 20–24, 35, 54, 63
Boni and Liveright, 121
Book of Mormon, passages in Humanist Press edition, 172
Boyd, Julian, 12
Buchanan, James, 84
Buddhist scriptures, passages in Humanist Press edition, 172, 174–75
Calvin, John, 176
Carr, Peter, 26–30, 60

Christianity: Bolingbroke's criticism of, 22–23; claims that US was founded on, 166–67; Jefferson on reason and free enquiry about, 26; Jefferson's defense of his version, 48; Priestley's approach to, 32, 35, 54; Virginia law punishing dissent from, 15–16
Christian nationalists, 167
Church, Forrest, 142–46
Church, Frank, 142, 145
Clarkson N. Potter, 148
Clay, Charles, 44–47
Cochran, Joseph, 109
Cohen, Joshua I., 80–82, 124
Congress: edition of 1904 distributed to, 11, 135–37, 138–39, 142–43, 145–46, 172; funding the printing of *Life and Morals*, 102–5
Congressional Library: burned by the British, 40; Jefferson's sale of his books to, 40–43, 44, 47
conservation of Jefferson's original book, 12, 179–84
correspondence of Jefferson: with Adams, 6, 38–39, 40, 81, 82, 89, 170; with Clay, 44–47; mentioning execution of Servet, 177; with nephew Peter Carr, 26–30, 60; selectively quoted, 8; with Short, 50–54, 69, 71

Cotton States International
Exposition, 86–92
creation of *Life and Morals*:
books used for cutting and
pasting, 8, 37, 49, 81–82, 88,
124, 181–83, figure 4 at 189;
choices made in, 165; Clay's
warning about, 44–47;
compared to archaeological
excavation, 6–7, 179; contradictions of laws of nature
and, 27, 64; cutting and
pasting in, 10, 89; Jefferson's
confidence in, 57; with little
regard for original intentions, 8; *Philosophy of Jesus* as
preliminary to, 38–40, 48,
49; physical materials used
for, 180–81; plan confided to
Priestley and Rush, 36–37;
sorting the genuine from the
"rubbish," 6, 38, 50, 52–54,
156; unused clippings left
over from, 181–83
Cryer, Dan, 143, 144, 145
Cuban Missile Crisis, 148–49,
156
"cult" vs. "creed," at National
Museum, 79, 86, 91–92

Declaration of Independence,
25, 128–29, 133, 134
De heretico comburendo, 15
deism: ascribed to Jefferson, 150;
ascribed to Jews by Jefferson,
48; Christian criticism of,
44; indifferent to Christian
moral teachings, 35; of philosophers in Jefferson's
library, 41; of Reimarus, 58
Dewey, John, 119
*Die Jefferson-Bibel, Der wahre
Kern des Neuen Testaments,*
177–78
disciples. *See* followers of Jesus
Donnelly, Clarence Shirley, 153
Douglas, William, 17–18

Eakins Press, 161
editions of Jefferson Bible, 8,
11–13; digital, 176; fairly
cheap to produce, 149; first
commercial editions, 113–16;
first scholarly treatment, 12;
German, 177–78; highlighting Jefferson's religious bona
fides, 151; of Humanist Press,
172–76; inclusion of the
supernatural in, 115–16; Jackson's transformed text, 121–
24, 125–33; of Lurton, 138–
42; of National Museum of
American History in 2011,
12; in political turmoil of
1960s and 70s, 12, 157, 162,
170, 171; Spanish, 176–77;
with Unitarian ministers' introductions, 12, 146, 148, 149,
154–61. *See also* Government
Printing Office edition
Ellis, Janice Stagnitto, 180
Engel v. Vitale, 152

Enlightenment ideals: applied
by Jefferson to *The Life and
Morals*, 6, 69, 169, 176; of
Bolingbroke, 20, 22; culture
of young United States and,
10; of eighteenth- and early
nineteenth-century biographers of Jesus, 61; Harrington's attunement to, 148;
Jefferson's youthful exposure
to, 16, 20, 22

First Amendment, Establishment Clause of, 152
Fisk, James, 42–43
The Five Gospels (Funk and
Hoover), 55, 57
followers of Jesus: accused by
Jefferson of injury to his doctrines, 7, 35–36, 38, 52, 53, 59–
60, 170, 173; accused by
Reimarus of conscious fraud,
59–60; recasting his death as
a victory, 59
forgiveness of sin, 51, 69, 70–71,
72. *See also* redemption;
repentance; salvation
founding fathers, and religion,
10, 151
freedom: Harrington on fear
in atomic age and, 159; interest in Lurton's edition
and, 141; Jackson's version of
Jefferson Bible and, 121–22,
129, 133. *See also* religious
liberty

French language, used in Jefferson's project, 10, 18, 48, 49
Funk, Robert, 55, 56, 57, 59, 60

Gale, Zona, 119
Galileo Galilei, 31
Gaustad, Edwin, 16, 19
German edition of *Jefferson
Bible*, 177–78
God: Bolingbroke's criticism of
Bible version of, 23, 24;
Christian vs. deist, 44 (*see
also* deism); Jefferson's advice
to his nephew and, 26, 29;
Jefferson's God of nature,
24–25, 44; Virginia law pun-
ishing forbidden beliefs
about, 15–16
The Gospel Coalition (online
portal), 171
Gospel of Thomas, 55
Gospel writers. *See* followers of
Jesus; Matthew; Mark;
Luke; John
Government Printing Office
edition: as 1904 facsimile of
the original, 11, 179–80;
Adler's introduction to, 11,
102, 106, 109–10, 116–17; bill
passed by Congress, 105; in
cornerstone of Jefferson
Memorial, 134–35; custom of
presenting to Congress-
members, 142, 172; demand
for initial 9,000 copies, 135–
37; as first correct edition,

115–16; Lacey's proposal for, 102–5, 112, 113, 116; of Lurton's father, 138–41; opposition after congressional approval, 105–13; passed down through the generations, 11, 137, 138–39, 142–43, 145–46; for sale on eBay, 146; title page of, 116–17

Granados, Luis, 172, 173

Greek language, used in Jefferson's project, 10, 18, 37, 48, 49

Grosvenor, Charles H., 103, 104

Harrington, Donald, 147–49, 154–61

healing: edition with illustrations of, 151; of the man with a withered hand, 67–68; publisher's inadvertent inclusion of, 114–16

Heatwole, Joel, 111–12

Hebrew Bible: Jefferson's advice to his nephew and, 27–28; passages in Humanist Press edition, 172, 173–74

Hemings, Sally, 168, 184

Henderson, David B., 103

Henry, J. Addison, 109

Herder, Johann Gottfried, 60

heresy: Adler's removal of name from title page and, 117; as crime with dire consequences, 15–16; disagreements about Jefferson's work and, 165–66; faculty oath at College of William and Mary and, 19; Jefferson's turn toward, 7, 117, 151, 184; literal Greek meaning of, 165; Priestley accused of, 34. See also atheism; blasphemy

Hess, Johann Jakob, 60

A History of the Corruptions of Christianity (Priestley), 32

Hoover, Roy, 55

Huch, Tobias, 177–78

Huckabee, Mike, 166

Humanist Press edition, 172–76

immaculate conception, 64, 143

incarnation: Bolingbroke on, 23; minister's condemnation of publication and, 108

"Indians," Life and Morals supposedly prepared for, 39, 85

Jackson, Henry: beginning a publishing program, 120–21; launching College of Social Engineering, 118–20, 128, 132; melding Gospels with American ideals, 121–22, 126–27, 128–29; publishing transformed version of Jefferson Bible, 121–24, 125–33; testifying on Social Security Act, 133

Jakobi, Johann Adolph, 60

Jefferson, Peter, 18

Jefferson, Thomas: biblical scholars' dedication of book

Jefferson, Thomas (*continued*)
to, 55; death of his father, 18;
early reconsiderations of Jesus's life and, 58–63; Enlightenment ideals and, 6, 16, 20,
22, 69, 148, 169, 176; enslaved
people and, 1, 16, 168; hairs
found among pages of Life
and Morals, 183–84; heresy
associated with, 7, 117, 151,
184; interested in science, 19,
155; with no intention to
publish his project, 7, 47, 48,
73; prayer and Bible-reading
in schools and, 152–54; religious upbringing of, 16–18;
selling his books to Con-
gress, 40–43, 44, 47; suspected of atheism, 34, 41, 42,
43–44, 45, 127. *See also* correspondence of Jefferson
Jefferson Bible: becoming a new
religious expression in 1960s,
162–64; in cornerstone of
Jefferson Memorial, 134–35;
illuminating changing public
opinion, 5, 9–10; *Life and
Morals of Jesus of Nazareth*
transformed into, 75, 89; as a
life's work, 54; as many
books, not only *Life and
Morals*, 8–9; objections to
calling it *Jefferson Bible*, 9. *See
also* editions of *Jefferson
Bible*; *Life and Morals of Jesus
of Nazareth*

*The Jefferson Bible for the
Twenty-First Century* (Humanist Press edition), 172–76
The Jefferson Lies (Barton),
168–71, 175
*Jefferson's Extracts from the
Gospels* (first scholarly
edition), 12, 39
Jesus: early reconsiderations of
the life of, 58–63; followers
of, 35–36, 52, 53, 59–60, 170,
173; Jefferson's denial of divinity of, 33, 102; Jefferson's
statements of disagreements
with, 51, 52; as a man, 28, 33,
161, 162; as man of his times,
59, 61; Priestley's influence on
Jefferson's interpretation of,
32–33. *See also* moral teachings of Jesus
"Jesus Rejected at Nazareth"
(Luke 4:14–30), 125–27
Jesus Seminar, 55–57, 58, 59
"Jew Bill," 80
Jewish community: Cyrus
Adler's advocacy for, 75;
Government Printing Office
edition and, 110; Jesus's mission to end Roman oppres-
sion of, 59
John, Gospel of, 63, 69, 182
Johnson, Samuel, 20
John the Baptist, 71

Kennedy, Anthony, 167
Kennedy, John F., 148–49

Kennedy, Robert, 161
King, Martin Luther, Jr., 161
King James version, 87, 122, 123, 150
Kirk, Russell, 152–53
Knox, Ronald, 150

Lacey, John Fletcher: as admirer of Jefferson, 101–2; childhood interest in religion, 99–101; photo of, figure 6 at 191; promoting publication of Life and Morals, 102–5, 112, 113, 116; supposed discovery of *Jefferson Bible* by, 95–99
Latin language, used in Jefferson's project, 10, 18, 48, 49
laws of nature: Jefferson's college education about, 19; Jefferson's methodology and, 27, 28, 64; Reimarus and, 58
The Life and Morals of Jesus of Nazareth: 200th anniversary of completion, 9; Adler's view of religious liberty and, 93–94; agenda-driven reframings of, 172, 175–76; almost unknown for much of nineteenth century, 73, 74; at Atlanta exposition in 1895, 86–92; birth, naming, and youth of Jesus in, 63, 64–66; Christian tropes avoided by, 64; Church's Master's thesis on, 144; edition used in

quoting from, 12; excisions at cost of popular appeal, 67–72; languages used in, 10, 18, 48, 49; last words of, 72; omitting first chapter of each Gospel, 63, 65; reactions contrary to Jefferson's intentions, 150–51; read each night by Jefferson, 7, 74, 83, 127, 184; as a remix, 8; roughly one thousand verses in, 10; as title used by Jefferson, 5, 9; transformed into *Jefferson Bible*, 75, 89. *See also* creation of *Life and Morals; Jefferson Bible*; original book of *Life and Morals*
Life of Jesus (Strauss), 61–63
"Literary Commonplace Book" of Jefferson, 20
Locke, John, 19
love, Harrington on, 157, 159, 160
Luke, Gospel of, 63, 66, 70–71, 125–27
Lurton, Douglas, 12, 138–42

Madison, James, 43, 47
Mark, Gospel of, 63, 71, 182–83
Marty, Martin, 150
Matthew, Gospel of, 63, 67–68, 71–72, 114–15, 182
Maury, James, 18
McKay, David, 116
miraculous and supernatural elements: Barton's *Jefferson Lies* and, 169; Church's

miraculous and supernatural
  elements (*continued*)
  reaction to *Jefferson Bible*
  and, 143; edition with illustrations of, 151; Harrington's
  historical perspective on, 157;
  healing by Jesus, 67–68, 114–
  16, 151; humanist rejection of,
  173; McKay's edition with
  list of, 116; omitted by Jefferson, 10, 64, 66–69, 71–72,
  102, 150, 155–56, 183; opposition to Congress's publication and, 106, 107–8;
  Reimarus on, 58–59; Strauss's
  Life of Jesus and, 61, 62;
  Thompson's edition and, 114,
  115; unintended conse-
  quences of omitting, 67–69,
  71–72
Monacan people, 2, 4–5, 6
"Morals of Jesus," on cover of
  original book, 83, 85, 96, 159
moral teachings of Jesus:
  Bolingbroke on, 22, 24;
  Clay's warning to Jefferson
  and, 45–46; Harrington on,
  160; Jackson on duty and,
  130–31, 133; Jefferson's private
  laugh at his opponents and,
  40; King on people's response to, 161; in *Philosophy
  of Jesus*, 48; Priestley and, 35,
  37; separated from interpolations of biographers, 51–
  53; as sublime code for

Jefferson, 6, 36, 38, 47, 51, 53,
  81, 89, 141, 170
mounds. *See* barrows, excavation of
Murray v. Curlett, 152

museums of Smithsonian. *See*
  National Museum; National
  Museum of American
  History
nationalists, Christian, 167
National Museum, 10, 76–79,
  86, 91–92
National Museum of American
  History, 8, 12, 179–84
"nature's God," 25, 44
New English Bible, 150
New Testament: Jefferson's
  challenge to his nephew and,
  28–29; Jefferson's opinion of
  most of, 6; two copies mutilated by Jefferson, 37, 49, 81–
  82, 88, 124, 181–83, figure 4
  at 189. *See also* Bible
The New Testament in Modern
  Speech, 122. *See also* Weymouth New Testament
Newton, Isaac, 19
1960s America: Barton's enlist-
  ment in culture wars of, 170,
  171; editions viewed through
  political turmoil of, 12;
  Jefferson Bible becoming
  new religious expression in,
  162–64; search for spiritual
  solutions in, 157

Notes on the State of Virginia
(Jefferson), 1, 25–26
Nouveau testament, le, 49

Opitz, Ernst August, 60
original book of Life and
Morals: as 84-page volume,
10; Adler's discovery of, 84–
86; at Atlanta exposition in
1895, 86–92; conservation of,
12, 179–84; examined with
modern technology, 180–81;
exhibited in 2011 at National
Museum of American His-
tory, 12, 179, 180; hairs found
with, 183–84; now in collection of National Museum of
American History, 8; photos
of, following page 185; unused
clippings found with, 181–83
Overman, I. L., 109
Paine, Thomas, 168
Payne, Sereno, 104
Peacock, John, 109–10
The Philosophy of Jesus, 38–40,
48, 49
Potter, Clarkson N., 149
Powell, Adam Clayton, 162–64
Powers, Hiram, 100–101
prayer and Bible reading in
public schools, 151–54
Priestley, Joseph, 31–37, 54, 88,
124, 144, 148
Princeton University Press, 12
public disclosure: Jefferson's
avoidance of, 7, 73; by Jesus

Seminar, 57; Reimarus's
avoidance of, 60
Quran: in Jefferson's library, 41;
passages in Humanist Press
edition, 172, 174
Randall, Harry S., 17, 83
Randolph, Carolina Ramsey, 86
Randolph, Sarah, 85
Randolph, Thomas Jefferson, 84
reason: Bolingbroke on ethics
in New Testament and, 22,
24; Church's view of Jefferson and, 144; opinions on
Jefferson's Life and Morals
and, 5; Priestley's faith and,
32, 33–34
reason in Jefferson's thought:
advice to his nephew and,
26–27, 29–30; advocacy
against Anglican establishment and, 34; approach to
study of religion and, 41; college education and, 19; corruptions of Christianity and,
26; method for redaction
project and, 53, 65, 66, 70,
72, 135, 169; reconciliation
with religion, 155, 184
redemption: Bolingbroke on,
23; Church on Jefferson's
quest and, 144. See also forgiveness of sin; salvation
Reimarus, Hermann Samuel,
58–60, 62
Religion in the Age of Science
(Harrington), 148

religious authority: culture of young US and, 10; Jefferson on stifling nature of, 25–26

religious diversity: in American Humanist Association edition, 172–76; of Harrington's New York Community Church, 147, 154–55; Jefferson quoted on, 154

religious history, American, 10, 13, 146

religious liberty: Adler's statement on, 92–94; Jefferson's defense of, 34; of today's readers of Life and Morals, 178; Virginia statute on, 25, 153; Washington on, 93

religious persecution: of Priestley, 31, 34; punishment of heresy, 15–16

religious tradition: burying the Jesus of history, 6–7; Harrington's critical analysis of, 158; Jefferson's advice to his nephew and, 29; Jefferson's discomfort with accounts about Jesus and, 51; Jefferson's exposure to science and, 19; Jesus's teachings inseparable from, 72

repentance, 23, 51, 59, 69, 71

resurrection: Church's reaction to Jefferson Bible and, 143; King on Jesus's moral teachings and, 161, 162; omitted by Jefferson, 64, 72, 113, 150, 175;

opposition to publication by government and, 108, 113

Revised Standard Version of Bible, 149

Roosevelt, Franklin, Jr., 148

Roosevelt, Franklin D., 134–35

Roosevelt, Theodore, 75

Rush, Benjamin, 36–37, 51, 167

salvation: Christian opposition to deism and, 44; Harrington's interpretation of search for, 157; Jesus's suggestion that belief is sufficient for, 70–71; King on the appeal of, 161. See also forgiveness of sin; redemption

Schempp v. the School District of Abington Township, 152

Schweitzer, Albert, 58, 59, 60–61

science: Harrington on Christian dogma and, 158; Harrington on the nuclear threat and, 159; Jefferson's interest in, 19, 155

Second Great Awakening, 82

separation between church and state, 107, 147, 152

Servet, Migel, 176–77

Shaw, George Bernard, 161–62

Short, William, 50–54, 69, 71

Small, William, 19

Smithsonian Institution: Division of Religion, 75, 76–77 (see also Adler, Cyrus);

exhibit at Cotton States International Exposition, 86–92. *See also* National Museum; National Museum of American History

social engineering: concept of, 119–20; Jackson *on Jefferson Bible* and, 128, 130. *See also* Jackson, Henry

Socrates, Priestley's comparison of Jesus to, 35

Spanish edition of *Jefferson Bible*, 176–77

Spofford, Ainsworth R., 85, 95, 98

Stevens, Wallace, 99

Strauss, David, 61–63

Syllabus, 36–37, 51, 52

Thomas Jefferson Encyclopedia, 39

"Thomas Jefferson's Bible," so called by Adler, 88, 89, 90, 91, 92

Thomas Jefferson's Bible: Undiscovered Teachings of Jesus (Jackson), 121–24, 131

Thomas Jefferson's Human Jesus (Eakins Press edition), 161–62

Thomas Nelson & Sons, 149, 168, 171

Thompson, Charles, 48

Thompson, N. D., 113–15

Trinity: Jefferson's avoidance of, 64; Jefferson's early doubts about, 18–19; Priestley on, 32; Servet's execution for denying tradition of, 176–77; Virginia law punishing denial of, 16

Tupper, Kerr Boyce, 107–8

Unitarianism: Jefferson on, 146; of Priestley, 32, 33, 34, 144

Unitarian Universalist ministers, 12; Donald Harrington, 147–49, 154–61; Forrest Church, 142, 144–46

University of Virginia, absence of chapel at, 82–83

Vida y doctrinas de Jesus, 176–77

Vietnam War, 144, 161

Virginia laws against heresy, 15–16

Virginia Statute of Religious Freedom, 25, 153

Voltaire, 168

Washington, George, 93

Weymouth, Richard Francis, 122

Weymouth New Testament, 121, 122–23, 132

Wilfred Funk, Inc., 138

WND Books, 171

World Net Daily, 171

Wright, Robert, 43